Chartered Institute for Securities & Investment

Level 3

Certificate in Investment Administration (IAQ™)

Introduction to Securities and Investment

Practice and Revision Kit

July 2010

Syllabus version 10

BPP LEARNING MEDIA

Contents

A note about copyright

Dear Customer

What does the little © mean and why does it matter?

Your market-leading BPP books, course materials and e-learning materials do not write and update themselves. People write them: on their own behalf or as employees of an organisation that invests in this activity. Copyright law protects their livelihoods. It does so by creating rights over the use of the content.

Breach of copyright is a form of theft – as well being a criminal offence in some jurisdictions, it is potentially a serious beach of professional ethics.

With current technology, things might seem a bit hazy but, basically, without the express permission of BPP Learning Media:

- Photocopying our materials is a breach of copyright
- Scanning, ripcasting or conversion of our digital materials into different file formats, uploading them to facebook or emailing them to your friends is a breach of copyright

You can, of course, sell your books, in the form in which you have brought them – once you have finished with them. (Is this fair to your fellow students? We update for a reason.) But the e-products are sold on a single user license basis: we do not supply 'unlock' codes to people who have bought them second-hand.

And what about outside the UK? BPP Learning Media strives to make our materials available at prices students can afford by local printing arrangements, pricing policies and partnerships which are clearly listed on our website. A tiny minority ignore this and indulge in criminal activity by illegally photocopying out material or supporting organisations that do. If they act illegally and unethically in on area, can you really trust them?

Question Bank

Contents

1. Introduction to Financial Services and the Economic Environment

Questions

1. ✓ Which of the following measures the total value of goods and services produced within the UK?

   A   PSNCR
   Ⓑ   GDP
   C   CPI
   D   GDP deflator

2. ✓ Which one of these services would a third party administrator not provide?

   A   Consolidated reporting
   Ⓑ   Trade execution
   C   Custody
   D   International settlement

3. ✗ Which of the following statements is the least relevant to a market economy?

   Ⓐ   Facilitating international trade helps people's needs to be met.
   B   Markets are driven by levels of supply and demand.
   C   Economic growth is enhanced through central planning.
   D   The price mechanism is central to the allocation of resources.

4. ✓ Which one of the following statements is true of the public sector net cash requirement?

   A   It represents the net deficit on the UK's balance of payments
   B   It represents the total taxes collected by the government
   Ⓒ   It is funded through the issue of gilts
   D   It is a measure of inflation

5. ✓ Which of the following would not be included in GDP figures in the UK?

   I   Earnings from tourism
   II   Income generated by financial sector
   III   Work carried out on a property by its owner
   IV   Work carried out for cash in hand by a person on the unemployment register

   A   I, III and IV
   B   I and II
   Ⓒ   III and IV
   D   II and III

6. ✓ **Which of the following statements is true?**

   A   The Monetary Policy Committee sets inflation

   B   Falling retail sales would indicate inflationary pressure in the economy

   C   Tourism is not part of the balance of payments

   Ⓓ   The RPI includes mortgage payments

7. ✗ **Which one of the following sentences best describes the function of a custodian?**

   Ⓐ   A firm that deals and settles on an investor's behalf and then holds the security in title

   B   A firm that offers settlement and corporate action processing services to investors

   C   A firm that simply credits security income to an investor's account on the contracted date

   D   A firm that invests clients' money on a discretionary basis

8. ✗ **Which of the following own the London Stock Exchange?**

   A   The Bank of England

   B   The Financial Services Authority

   C   Its shareholders

   Ⓓ   Its exchange officials

9. ✓ **Which one of the following features is true of ICE Futures?**

   A   It is the trading platform for commodity derivatives

   B   It is owned by IEC

   Ⓒ   It is the trading platform for energy derivatives

   D   ICE futures is regulated by the SEC

10. ✓ **On which of the following exchanges can you trade US equities in euros?**

   Ⓐ   Deutsche Börse

   B   EUREX

   C   LIFFE

   D   Deutsche Terminbörse

11. ✓ **In the UK, how would you expect the current account to be shown in the balance of payments?**

   Ⓐ   Visibles in deficit, invisibles in surplus

   B   Visibles in deficit, invisibles in deficit

   C   Visibles in surplus, invisibles in deficit

   D   Visibles in surplus, invisibles in surplus

12. ✓ **Which of the following is not a function of the Bank of England?**

   A   Setting of interest rates via the MPC

   B   Maintaining stability in the financial system

   Ⓒ   Responsible for banking supervision

   D   Appointing the Chairman of the Panel on Takeovers and Mergers

13. ✓ **Which of the following exchanges is not part of NYSE Euronext?**

   A   Amsterdam

   Ⓑ   Berlin

   C   Paris

   D   Brussels

14. ✓ **Which one of the following would reduce the Public Sector Net Cash Requirement?**

   Ⓐ   Increasing corporate taxation

   B   Printing money

   C   Borrowing from abroad

   D   Selling Treasury bills to UK residents

15. ✓ **Which of the following represents a measure of inflation in the UK that is harmonised with European inflationary measures?**

   Ⓐ   CPI

   B   RPIX

   C   RPIY

   D   HIRP

16. ✓ **Which of the following is true of NASDAQ?**

   A   It is an order-driven market

   B   It is a market primarily for trading American derivatives

   Ⓒ   It is a market primarily for technology and innovative companies

   D   Only fully listed companies may trade on NASDAQ

17. ✓ **Which of the following are true statements about the Retail Prices Index?**

   | | I | It is a weighted index which reflects the cost of goods and services in the UK economy |

   I   It is a weighted index which reflects the cost of goods and services in the UK economy

   II   It excludes the effects of changes in mortgage interest payments

   III   It reflects changes in the inflation rate

   IV   If the RPI was 10% the value of money would halve in five years

   A   I and II

   Ⓑ   I and III

   C   I, II and III

   D   I, II and IV

18. ✓ **Spot Forex deals are normally settled within**

    A One business day

    Ⓑ Two business days

    C Three business days

    D Five business days

19. ✓ **Settlement for foreign currency forward deals is generally**

    A One business day

    B Two business days

    C Three business days

    Ⓓ The day agreed by the participants to the transaction

20. ✕ **The foreign exchange markets in the UK are dominated by**

    A Banks

    B Lloyd's of London

    Ⓒ Money brokers

    D Independent brokers

21. ✓ **A principal trade refers to a trade where**

    A The firm has priority over other firms when executing the deal

    B The trade is effected on behalf of a customer where the firm's remuneration is by way of commission

    Ⓒ The trade is effected by the firm on its own behalf and for its own account

    D The trade is the first undertaken during that day's trading

22. ✓ **UK equities can be traded on**

    Ⓐ LSE

    B NYSE LIFFE

    C ICE Futures

    D LME

23. ✓ **What is the name of the trade body for the UK asset management industry?**

    A Association of Investment Funds

    B Asset Management Institute

    C Association of UK Asset Managers

    Ⓓ Investment Management Association

Answers

1. **B** GDP or Gross Domestic Product. GNP or Gross National Product refers to goods and services produced by the nationals of a particular country

    See Sections 1.9.1 of your Study Text

2. **B** TPAs provide back office services, i.e. after the trade is done. Hence they would not execute trades for their clients

    See Section 3.11 of your Study Text

3. **B** Central planning of production is a feature of a State-controlled economy, while a market economy involves much less State intervention. In a market economy resource allocation determined is by the price mechanism, through the dynamic forces of supply and demand. Trade is one aspect of the free market, which generally enables people's needs to be met

    See Section 1.3 of your Study Text

4. **C** The balance of payments is the difference between imports and exports. PSNCR is the difference between government spending and tax revenues

    See Section 1.9.3 of your Study Text

5. **C** III and IV form part of the unofficial or black economy and thus are not part of the Gross Domestic Product calculation

    See Section 1.9.1 of your Study Text

6. **D** The MPC sets interest rates, not inflation. The inflation target is set by the Chancellor

    See Sections 1.8.1 and 2.2 of your Study Text

7. **B** Custodians generally offer safekeeping, settlement and corporate action processing services to their clients but do not normally deal for their clients. In other words, they do more than just credit a client's account with income on a contracted date. Custodians do not normally take investment decisions

    See Section 3.9 of your Study Text

8. **C** Since demutualisation, the LSE has been a plc and, like any other plc, is owned by its shareholders

    See Section 4.1 of your Study Text

9. **C** ICE Futures is for the trading of energy derivatives and is owned by the Inter-Continental Exchange (ICE)

    See Section 5.2 of your Study Text

10. **A** Deutsche Börse deals with securities. (Deutsche Terminbörse is the former name of Eurex.)

    See Section 6.5 of your Study Text

11. **A** Visible trade is trade conducted in physical goods; invisibles are trades in services and income flows

    See Section 1.9.2 of your Study Text

12.   **C**   It is the FSA that is responsible for banking supervision

See Section 2.1 of your Study Text

13.   **B**   NYSE Euronext is the second largest exchange in Europe behind the LSE

See Sections 5.1 and 6.2 of your Study Text

14.   **A**   Government spending over and above the money collected from taxation represents the PSNCR. Thus, if more money is collected by taxing businesses, the PSNCR will reduce

See Section 1.9.3 of your Study Text

15.   **A**   The Consumer Prices Index is a measure of consumer price inflation, calculated using methodology similar to that used in the rest of Europe

See Section 1.8.2 of your Study Text

16.   **C**   As one of the largest electronic quote-driven markets in the world, NASDAQ specialises in offering a trading platform for technology and innovative companies

See Section 6.3 of your Study Text

17.   **B**   The RPI is a weighted index which reflects changes in the rate of inflation. Unlike RPIX, the RPI includes mortgage interest payments unless it is RPIX

See Section 1.8.1 of your Study Text

18.   **B**   Remember that these are business days not calendar days

See Section 7.2 of your Study Text

19.   **D**   Each forward is tailored to suit the counterparties' needs, hence there is no fixed settlement date – parties agree a dare unique to that forward transaction

See Section 7.3 of your Study Text

20.   **A**   The large and informal forex markets are dominated by the major banks

See Section 7.1 of your Study Text

21.   **C**   Sometimes this is called proprietary trading

See Section 4.3 of your Study Text

22.   **A**   LIFFE is for the trading of futures and options of shares, while ICE Futures is for the trading of energy derivative products. The LME is for trading metal derivatives

See Sections 4.1 and 4.3 of your Study Text

23.   **D**   The IMA is the trade body for the UK asset management industry.

See Section 3.11 of your Study Text

2. Asset Classes

Questions

1. ✓ **What is the best description of the role of a market maker?**

   A   Deals as an agent for a customer

   Ⓑ   Buys and sells for the firm during the Mandatory Quote Period

   C   Arranges mergers and acquisitions

   D   Arranges new issues

2. ✓ **Which of the following is true of CREST?**

   A   It provides for confirmation of trades

   Ⓑ   It provides for delivery versus payment

   C   It is owned and operated by the Bank of England

   D   It only offers facilities for both dematerialised and paper settlement

3. ✗ **What is the next coupon payment for an investor holding Treasury 8% 2015 if it is trading at £134?**

   A   £4.00

   Ⓑ   £3.70

   C   £7.40

   D   £8.00

4. ✓ **Which of the following is another name for UK government bonds?**

   Ⓐ   Gilt-edged securities

   B   Loan stock

   C   Corporate bonds

   D   National Savings & Investments

5. ✗ **A loan is approaching redemption at par value shortly. Which of the following is likely to be the price?**

   A   Much higher than par

   B   Close to par

   C   Much lower than par

   Ⓓ   Any of the above

6. ✓ **LIBOR means**

   Ⓐ London Interbank Offered Rate

   B London Interbank Open Rate

   C London International Bank Offered Rate

   D London Internal Bank Offered Rate

7. ⚹ **Which of the following provides book entry facilities for equities?**

   A Euroclear UK & Ireland

   Ⓑ SETS

   C SEAQ

   D MarketMatch

8. ✓ **Which one of the following is true of Eurobonds?**

   A They can only be issued in a European currency

   Ⓑ New issues are through syndicates of banks

   C They are usually in registered form

   D A medium-term bond is called a FRA

9. ✓ **Which one of the following is not an advantage of investing in gilts?**

   A The credit rating of the UK Government

   B Potential tax-free gains

   C A regular income stream

   Ⓓ A rise in value as interest rates rise

10. ✓ **What is the settlement period for fixed interest stocks?**

    A T + 1

    Ⓑ T + 3

    C T + 5

    D T + 10

11. ✓ **Which measure is used as the base to fix the interest rate for a FRN?**

    A RPI

    Ⓑ LIBOR

    C FTSE Index

    D APR

12. What is SETS?

Ⓐ A trading system

B A settlement system for overseas equities

C An electronic trade confirmation system

D A news dissemination system

13. Which of the following is not a function of Euroclear UK & Ireland, which operates CREST?

Ⓐ It creates payment obligations

B It automatically reconciles members' holdings of stock

C It arranges settlement of registered securities

D It notifies the company registrar that settlement has taken place

14. During which hours will SETS have automatic execution?

A 8:00-17:15

Ⓑ 8:30-17:30

C 8:50-16:30

D 8:00-16:30

15. On which trading platform are fixed interest securities traded?

Ⓐ SEAQ

B SETS

C SETSqx

D CREST

16. How many market makers must there be in SEAQ securities?

Ⓐ At least one

B At least two

C At least three

D At least four

17. Which of the following is not one of the participants you would expect to find in the CREST system?

A Sponsored member

Ⓑ Service member

C User member

D Market maker

18. ✓ **Settlement for Eurobonds is usually**

    A The business day following the day of dealing

    B The second business day following the day of dealing

    Ⓒ The third business day following the day of dealing

    D Seven calendar days

19. ✓ **The difference between the buying and selling price of a share is known as**

    A Bid

    Ⓑ Spread

    C Touch

    D Offer

20. ✓ **Settlement in UK equity transactions usually takes place via**

    Ⓐ Euroclear UK & Ireland

    B Clearstream

    C The Bank of New York

    D Euroclear

21. ✗ **Which is the best definition of a Eurobond?**

    A A French company issuing a €-denominated bond in France

    Ⓑ A French company issuing a €-denominated bond in US

    C A French company issuing a $-denominated bond in France

    D A French company issuing a $-denominated bond in US

22. ✓ **Which of the following is another name for equities?**

    A Bonds

    B Gilts

    Ⓒ Shares

    D Warrants

23. ✓ **Which of the following is not a type of order on SETS?**

    A Limit

    B At best

    C Fill or kill

    Ⓓ Auction

24. Which of the following is not a type of money market instrument?

A Treasury bill

B Corporate bond

C Commercial paper

D Commercial bill

25. The FTSE 100 Index comprises the 100 largest companies measured by reference to

A Profit

B Market capitalisation

C Turnover

D Share price

26. What are a company's Memorandum and Articles of Association?

    I   The Memorandum deals with the company's relationship with the outside world

    II   The Articles deal with the company's relationship with the outside world

    III   The Articles deal with the internal relationships within the company

    IV   They are the same as the company's prospectus

A II and IV

B I and IV

C I and III

D IV only

27. In what way is investing in preference shares similar to investing in bonds?

A Have equal security in event of a winding up

B Dividends on preference shares are usually fixed

C Both must give the same return

D Both have equal voting rights

28. Which of the following issues raise funds for the company?

    I   Rights

    II   Scrip

    III   Capitalisation

    IV   Loan stock

A I and IV

B II and III

C I and III

D I, II and III

29. ✓ **Calculate the next coupon payment for Treasury 5½% 2012 trading at £103.**

    Ⓐ £2.75

    B £5.30

    C £5.50

    D £100

30. ✓ **What are the two alternative names for a bonus issue?**

    I   Scrip

    II   Capitalisation

    III Premium

    IV Rights

    Ⓐ I and II

    B III and IV

    C II and III

    D I and III

31. ✓ **Which of the following is not usually underwritten?**

    A Rights issue

    B Offer for sale

    C Offer for subscription

    Ⓓ Deeply discounted rights issue

32. ✓ **If you buy a gilt, you must settle by the end of**

    Ⓐ The next business day

    B Two-week account system

    C Five business days

    D Three business days

33. ✓ **Which of the following sentences best describes price risk?**

    A It is the only source of risk when buying shares

    Ⓑ It is the risk of adverse price movements in the share

    C It is the risk of a company going into liquidation

    D It is the risk of a counterparty failing to pay its obligations

34. ✓ **Regarding SETS, which of the following is not a term used for a type of order?**

    Ⓐ Fixed price order

    B At best order

    C Fill or kill order

    D Execute and eliminate

35. ✗ **A client read in the newspaper named Funding 2012-2014 and asked you what this description means. You would reply that**

A   The gilt is redeemable at the option of the Government between dates in 2012 and 2014

B   The gilt is redeemable at the option of the Government at dates in 2012 or 2014

Ⓒ   The gilt is redeemable at the option of the investor between 2012 and 2014

D   The gilt is redeemable at the option of the investor in 2012 or 2014

36. ✓ **What is the standard settlement period for UK equities?**

A   Same day

B   T + 1

Ⓒ   T + 3

D   T + 5

37. ✗ **Classify the following gilt according to the DMO classifications: Treasury 5% 2014, issued in 1989**

A   Short dated

B   Medium dated

Ⓒ   Long dated

D   Undated

38. ✓ **On a government stock dated 2012-2015, which of the following is true?**

I   Redemption has to take place in 2012

II   The Government can redeem between 2012-2015

III   The stock will be index-linked

IV   Government can redeem at anytime if the coupon is less than interest rates

A   I, II, III and IV

Ⓑ   II only

C   III only

D   II and III

39. ✓ **The most likely reason to issue gilts is that the Government**

A   Needs to fund a current account deficit

Ⓑ   Needs to fund the PSNCR

C   Needs to control inflation

D   Wishes to win votes at the forthcoming General Election

40. ✓ **Which is always true of FRNs?**

A   They are long dated

B   They are short dated

Ⓒ   They pay floating rate interest

D   They pay fixed rate interest

41. Which of the following is not a benefit of owning shares?

   (A) Potential capital gains

   B Right to seize assets in the event of liquidation of the company

   C The right to vote at the company's AGM

   D The right to subscribe for new shares in the company when a rights issue is announced

42. The FTSE 250 Index measures the performance (in terms of capitalisation) of

   (A) The top 250 companies on the London Stock Exchange

   B The top 250 companies in Europe excluding the UK

   C The 250 companies beneath the top 100 on the London Stock Exchange

   D The top 250 companies in Europe including the UK

43. Which is the main index used to gauge the performance of UK shares?

   A FTSE Industrial Index

   B RPI

   (C) FTSE 100

   D Dow Jones Industrial Average

44. Which of the following indices represent the second largest group of listed plcs in the UK?

   A FTSE Ordinary

   B FTSE 100

   (C) FTSE 250

   (D) FTSE 350

45. Which of the following are true of an AGM?

      I   It must be held twice a year

      II   A shareholder can appoint a proxy to attend and vote

      III Most resolutions need a simple voting majority

      IV A company does not need shareholder permission to repurchase its own shares

   A I, II and III

   (B) II and III

   C I, II and IV

   D I, III and IV

46. What is the minimum percentage of votes that allows shareholders to pass a special resolution?

   (A) 100%

   B 75%

   C 25%

   D 50%

47. ✓ **How often must a company hold an AGM?**

    A   Every six months

    Ⓑ Every calendar year

    C   Every 15 months

    D   Every two years

48. ☀ **Which one of the following would not be included in a company's Memorandum of Association?**

    A   Statutory objectives

    B   Company's name

    C   Share capital

    Ⓓ Company's trading objectives

49. ✓ **A Treasury 4½% 2013 bond trades at a market value of £107.95. What is the flat yield?**

    A   4.5%

    B   3.1%

    C   5.4%

    Ⓓ 4.2%

50. ✓ **Which one of the following is not a UKLA rule for admission to the full list of the LSE?**

    A   All securities issued must be freely transferable

    B   The company must have a trading record of at least three years

    Ⓒ The shares must be sufficiently marketable, meaning that 15% of the company's capital is in the hands of the public

    D   The expected market value of shares issued must be at least £700,000

51. ✓ **With respect to the UKLA Listing Rules, which one of the following is not a requirement for admission to the full list of the LSE?**

    A   The expected market value of shares issued by the company must be at least £700,000

    B   All securities issued must be freely transferable

    Ⓒ The company must have a track record of at least five years

    D   There must be at least 25% of the company's share capital available for public purchase

52. ✓ **With respect to the UKLA Listing Rules, which one of the following is not a requirement for admission to the full list of the LSE?**

    Ⓐ The expected market value of shares issued by the company must be at least £200,000

    B   All securities issued must be freely transferable

    C   The company must have a track record of at least three years

    D   There must be at least 25% of the company's share capital available for public purchase

53. With respect to the UKLA Listing Rules, which one of the following is **not** a requirement for admission to the full list of the LSE?

A The expected market value of shares issued by the company must be at least £700,000

B All securities issued must be freely transferable

C The company must have a track record of at least three years

D There must be at least 30% of the company's share capital available for public purchase

54. Which of the following securities is regarded as a bearer security?

A Shares

B Gilts

C Corporate bonds

D Eurobonds

55. What is the income yield of a Treasury 5% gilt, redeemable in two years, trading at a market price of £98.50?

A 5.1%

B 5.0%

C 6.2%

D 6.8%

56. What is the flat yield of a Treasury 8% gilt, redeemable in five years, trading at a market price of £117.30?

A 8.0%

B 5.8%

C 4.0%

D 6.8%

57. What is the flat yield of a 6% corporate bond, redeemable in ten years, trading at a market price of £109.50?

A 8.0%

B 5.4%

C 5.5%

D 6.8%

58. What is the flat yield of a 4% corporate bond, redeemable in seven years, trading at a market price of £93?

A 7.0%

B 2.3%

C 4.0%

D 4.3%

59. ✓ **A convertible bond is so-called normally because**

    A   It is redeemable in more than one currency

    B   It is a derivative that is generally settled in cash

    Ⓒ   It is convertible to equity

    D   It can be re-based and converted to a zero coupon bond

Answers

1. **B**   Market makers are there to promote liquidity and efficiency in the market and hence constantly buy and sell stock during the MQP

    See Sections 8.2 and 8.4 of your Study Text

2. **B**   CREST is owned by Euroclear UK & Ireland, not the Bank of England. It can facilitate both dematerialised and paper settlement but offers a number of other services; including corporate actions processing

    See Section 9 of your Study Text

3. **A**   The next coupon payment may be calculated using the following formula. (The current market price is irrelevant)

    Nominal value × Coupon rate × 0.5   = £100 × 8% × 0.5 = £4

    Remember that all gilts except 2½% Consol pay coupons semi-annually. Hence, the 'next' coupon is half the annual coupon

    See Section 10.2.4 of your Study Text

4. **A**   National Savings & Investments forms part of Government borrowings, but UK Government bonds are specifically known as gilts

    See Section 10.1 of your Study Text

5. **B**   As a bond approaches the date on which it will be redeemed at par, the market price will get nearer to par

    See Section 10.2 of your Study Text

6. **A**   The definition of LIBOR is often examined

    See Section 12.1 of your Study Text

7. **A**   Book entry facilities mean dematerialised settlement. Euroclear UK & Ireland operates CREST, which will electronically settle many types of securities, including equities

    See Section 9.1 of your Study Text

8. **B**   Eurobonds may be in any currency. Variable interest bonds are known as Floating Rate Notes (FRNs). Any debt instrument of medium maturity is usually called a note

    See Section 11.2 of your Study Text

9. **D**   Remember, as interest rates rise the price of gilts and bonds, in general, will fall

    See Section 10.5 of your Study Text

10. **B**   Most trades settle T + 3 except for spot forex (T + 2) and gilts (T + 1). This question assumes that corporate bonds and eurobonds are the fixed interest stocks being discussed

    See Sections 10.2 and 11 of your Study Text

11. **B**   A FRN is a floating rate note, and the floating rate of interest is given by the London Interbank Offered Rate (LIBOR)

    See Section 11.1 of your Study Text

12.   **A**   SETS is an electronic trading platform of the London Stock Exchange

See Section 7.1 of your Study Text

13.   **B**   Reconciliations are not automatic but happen on a regular basis

See Section 9 of your Study Text

14.   **D**   The period between 08:00 and 16:30 is also known as Normal Market Hours

See Section 7.1 of your Study Text

15.   **A**   SEAQ is the London Stock Exchange's service for the fixed interest (bond) market and AIM securities that are not traded on either SETS or SETSqx

See Section 8 of your Study Text

16.   **B**   At least two, to ensure that there is some competition between market makers

See Section 8 of your Study Text

17.   **D**   All are participants except market makers

See Section 9.4 of your Study Text

18.   **C**   Eurobond settlement falls into the international settlement norm of T + 3

See Sections 11.1 and 11.2 of your Study Text

19.   **B**   The spread enables market makers to make profits: they buy in shares at a low price, generally reselling them into the market at a higher price

See Section 8.4 of your Study Text

20.   **A**   The bulk of equity trades will settle through Euroclear UK & Ireland (CREST), although there are other settlement systems, and inter-office settlement

See Section 9.1 of your Study Text

21.   **C**   Note both B and C meet the criteria for Eurobonds, i.e. the country the bond is issued in and the currency of issue are not aligned. However, C is much more likely to happen

See Section 11.2 of your Study Text

22.   **C**   Ordinary shareholders have equal voting rights and an equal right to participate in a dividend should one be declared

See Section 1.5 of your Study Text

23.   **D**   The five types of order on SETS are limit, at best, execute and eliminate, fill or kill, and market orders

See Section 7.3 of your Study Text

24.   **B**   A corporate bond would be a long-term investment, whereas money market instruments are usually short-term

See Section 12 of your Study Text

25. **B** FTSE 100 includes the top 100 UK companies by market capitalisation (Share price × Number of shares). The FTSE 100 represents approximately 70% of the UK market by value

See Sections 6.1 and 6.2 of your Study Text

26. **C** The Memorandum is the company's rules on external relationships, while the Articles govern the internal relationships of the company

See Section 1.2 of your Study Text

27. **B** The dividend on preference shares are usually fixed, as are the coupons on most bonds, unless of course they are floating rate

See Section 1.6 of your Study Text

28. **A** Rights issues and loan stock issues raise funds for the company

See Sections 3.2, 3.3 and 11.1 of your Study Text

29. **A** The next coupon payment can be calculated as follows. The next coupon payment is half the annual coupon payment

Nominal value × Coupon rate × 0.5 = £100 × 5.5% × 0.5

= £2.75

See Section 10.2.4 of your Study Text

30. **A** Bonus issues are also known as capitalisation or scrip issues

See Section 3.2 of your Study Text

31. **D** Deeply discounted rights issues are not underwritten

See Section 3.4.3 of your Study Text

32. **A** Normally T + 1

See Section 10.2.5 of your Study Text

33. **B** Price risk is the primary source of market risk and arises due to adverse changes in the share price. (Bear in mind that a share buyer also faces liquidity and credit/counterparty risk)

See Section 2.2 of your Study Text

34. **A** The term 'fixed price order' is not used – it would be a limit order

See Section 7.3 of your Study Text

35. **A** The Government has the choice over which date to redeem the gilt

See Section 10.2 of your Study Text

36. **C** Equities settle at T + 3

See Section 9.2 of your Study Text

37. **A** Maturity is measured from today until maturity (2014) and thus it is short dated. The issue date is not relevant

See Section 10.4 of your Study Text

38.　**B**　The Government has the choice to redeem the stocks between the two dates that have been specified

See Section 10.2 of your Study Text

39.　**B**　The Government generally requests that the DMO issues gilts to fund the PSNCR, rather than simply print money or raise taxes

See Section 10.3 of your Study Text

40.　**C**　They may be short or long dated but they will pay floating rate interest

See Section 11.1 of your Study Text

41.　**B**　Ordinary shareholders will participate equally when a company is wound up – but only if any monies remain

See Sections 1.5 and 2.1 of your Study Text

42.　**C**　The FTSE 250 starts at the 101st largest company by market capitalisation and goes down to the 350th

See Section 6.2 of your Study Text

43.　**C**　Answer D refers to the US market, while the RPI measures inflation

See Section 6.2 of your Study Text

44.　**C**　The FTSE 250 represents 250 companies after the top 100 companies listed in the UK, which make up the FTSE 100

See Section 6.2 of your Study Text

45.　**B**　The AGM must be held annually. The company needs shareholder approval to buy back their own shares. Most resolutions are passed with a simple majority

See Section 1.3 of your Study Text

46.　**B**　Special resolutions usually affect shareholders' rights: hence 75% of shareholders need to agree

See Section 1.3 of your Study Text

47.　**B**　Annual General Meetings are normally held every 12 months, but they must be held every calendar year, with a maximum gap of 15 months between two AGMs

See Section 1.3 of your Study Text

48.　**A**　'Statutory objectives' is a term used in reference to the Financial Services Authority

See Sections 1.2.2 of your Study Text

49. **D** The flat yield is calculated as follows.

$$\text{Flat Yield} = \frac{\text{Gross coupon}}{\text{Market price}} \times 100$$

$$= \frac{£4.50}{£107.95} \times 100$$

$$= 4.2\% \text{ to 1 d.p.}$$

See Section 11.7 of your Study Text

50. **C** The listing rule suggests that at least 25% of the shares are available for public purchase. This is deemed 'sufficiently marketable'. In addition to these rules, the company agrees to be bound by the continuing obligations of the UKLA rules

See Section 4.3 of your Study Text

51. **C** The company must have a trading record of at least three years, and there should be three years of audited financial statements. In addition to the 'full list' listing rules, the company must agree to meet the continuing obligations of the UKLA Listing Rules. These include publishing information about significant transactions, notifying the LSE of dividend distributions, issuing financial statements as well as disclosure of price-sensitive information

See Section 4.3 of your Study Text

52. **A** The minimum market value of the shares should be at least £700,000. It is if the company issues debt, that the expected market value of debt is at least £200,000. In addition to the 'full list' listing rules, the company must agree to meet the continuing obligations of the UKLA rules

See Section 4.3 of your Study Text

53. **D** There must be at least 25% of the company's share capital available for public purchase. This is known as 'sufficient marketability'. In addition to the 'full list' listing rules, the company must agree to meet the continuing obligations of the UKLA rules

See Section 4.3 of your Study Text

54. **D** Eurobonds are generally regarded as 'bearer' securities, as there is no such register of legal ownership held by the issuer. Therefore the 'bearer' of the security is the rightful legal owner. Shares, gilts and corporate bonds are regarded as 'registered' securities, as there is a register identifying legal ownership

See Section 2.3 of your Study Text

55. **A** The flat yield (also known as the income yield) is calculated by dividing the annual coupon (in cash terms) by the market price of the bond. Therefore:

£5 coupon/£98.50 price × 100 = 5.1% return

i.e. for an investment of £98.50, the investor will receive an annual coupon of £5 (gross), which is an effective return on his money of 5.1%

See Section 11.7 of your Study Text

56. **D**   The flat yield (also known as the income yield) is calculated by dividing the annual coupon (in cash terms) by the market price of the bond. Therefore:

£8 coupon/£117.30 price × 100 = 6.8% return

i.e. for an investment of £117.30, the investor will receive an annual coupon of £8 (gross), which is an effective return of his money of 6.8%

See Section 11.7 of your Study Text

57. **C**   The flat yield is calculated by dividing the annual coupon (in cash terms) by the market price of the bond. Therefore:

£6 coupon/£109.50 price × 100 = 5.48% return

i.e. for an investment of £110, the investor will receive an annual coupon of £6 (gross), which is an effective return of his money of 5.5% (rounded up)

See Section 11.7 of your Study Text

58. **D**   The flat yield is calculated by dividing the annual coupon (in cash terms) by the market price of the bond. Therefore:

£4 coupon/£93 price × 100 = 4.3% return

i.e. for an investment of £93, the investor will receive an annual coupon of £4 (gross), which is an effective return of his money of 4.3%

See Section 11.7 of your Study Text

59. **C**   Such a bond is normally convertible to equity.

See Section 11.6 of your Study Text

3. Derivatives

Questions

1. In which market conditions does the holder of a put option seek to profit?

   A Static market

   B Falling market

   C Volatile market

   D Rising market

2. Which of the following best describes the maximum rewards and risks for the writer of a call option?

   A Unlimited profit and unlimited loss

   B Limited profit and limited loss

   C Unlimited profit and limited loss

   D Limited profit and unlimited loss

3. An investor looking to secure a minimum sale price for his assets, but still leave potential for further profit would

   A Buy a call option

   B Buy a put option

   C Buy a future

   D Sell a future

4. Which of the following is the best definition of a future?

   A An obligation to buy a given quantity of an asset on a range of future dates at a predetermined price

   B An agreement to buy or sell a standard quantity of a specified asset on a fixed future date at a price agreed today

   C An agreement to buy or sell a standard quantity of a specified asset on a fixed future date at a price agreed in the future

   D The right to buy or sell a standard quantity of a specified asset on a fixed future date at a price agreed today

5. The writer of a put option

   A Expects the share price to fall

   B Expects the share price to rise

   C Will have to return the premium if the option is unexercised

   D Pays the premium

6. ✗ **Which one of the following statements is false with regard to options?**

    A Call options give the holder the right to buy the underlying share at the prevailing market price at a given date

    B A put option could be bought if an investor held the view that market prices were likely to fall

    C Holders of options pay the premium when opening the position

    Ⓓ Writers of options are generally looking for price stability

7. ✗ **Which one of the following statements concerning the buyer of an interest rate swap is true?**

    Ⓐ A floating rate is swapped for a floating rate

    B A fixed rate is swapped for a floating rate

    Ⓒ A floating rate is swapped for a fixed rate

    D Both parties make gross payments

8. ✗ **Which of the following trades is most risky?**

    A Long future

    B Short future

    Ⓒ Long call

    D Short put

9. ✓ **How much does the buyer of an option pay to acquire the right under the option?**

    Ⓐ The premium

    B The strike or exercise price

    C The full nominal value of the contract

    D The tick value for the contract

10. ✓ **What is meant by a 'call'?**

    A The obligation to buy a security at a set price

    B The obligation to sell a security at an unknown price

    Ⓒ The right to buy a security at a set price

    D The right to sell a security at a set price

11. ✗ **Selling a put option means you have the**

    A Right to buy

    Ⓑ Right to sell

    C Obligation to buy

    D Obligation to sell

12. If a put option is exercised, what is the maximum loss to the seller?

    A   Unlimited

    B   Premium + Exercise price

    C   Premium – Exercise price

    (D) Premium

13. Which of the following applies in respect of buying a future?

    A   Obligation to pay seller and deliver underlying

    (B) Obligation to deliver underlying and receive proceeds

    C   Obligation to receive underlying only

    D   Obligation to receive underlying and pay seller

14. Which option has unlimited potential losses?

    A   Long put

    B   Short put

    (C) Long call

    D   Short call

15. Able Limited writes a put option. What would best describe the company's position?

    A   Right to buy shares

    B   Obliged to buy if option buyer requests

    (C) Right to sell the share

    D   Obliged to sell if option buyer requests

16. Which of the following has unlimited risk of losses?

    (A) Writer of a call option

    B   Holder of a call option

    C   Writer of a put option

    D   Holder of a put option

17. What is the amount the buyer of traded options pays upon the purchase of the contract known as?

    A   Collateral

    (B) Premium

    C   Open interest

    D   Cash

Answers

1. **B** Holders also need volatility, but B is the best answer for the put buyer

   See Section 3.3.3 of your Study Text

2. **D** The profit is limited to the premium. When you are the writer of a call the potential loss is unlimited. Answer B would be the correct answer for the writer of a put

   See Section 3.3.2 of your Study Text

3. **B** With the put option, where the share price falls, the investor would exercise the put option, and sell the assets, at the exercise price. However, if the underlying share price rises, the investor would simply not exercise his option and keep the asset. If the share price were to rise, and the investor had sold a future, losses would result

   See Section 3.3.3 of your Study Text

4. **B** Answer D is a description of options

   See Section 2.1 of your Study Text

5. **B** A writer always receives a premium. The writer of a put will be expecting the price to rise so that the put option will not be exercised against them

   See Section 3.3.4 of your Study Text

6. **A** A call option is the right to buy at a predetermined price, not the prevailing price

   See Sections 3.2 and 3.3 of your Study Text

7. **B** Payments are netted down, so only one party makes a payment. The buyer pays 'fixed' and receives 'floating'

   See Section 5 of your Study Text

8. **B** Long Call – risk is premium. Long future and short put – risk is large but limited. Short future – risk is unlimited

   See Section 4 of your Study Text

9. **A** The price paid for an option is known as the premium on the option

   See Section 3.2 of your Study Text

10. **C** A call is the right, but not the obligation, of the holder to purchase the underlying at a price agreed at the outset

    See Section 3.2 of your Study Text

11. **C** The writer of a put option has the obligation to buy the underlying if the holder exercises the option. This is better described as a potential obligation

    See Section 3.3 of your Study Text

12. **C** The premium offsets the loss against the exercise price

    See Section 3.3.4 of your Study Text

13. **D** The buyer will pay the seller and receive the underlying if the contract goes to delivery

   See Section 2.1 of your Study Text

14. **D** The seller of a call has an unlimited potential loss and the upside is only the premium paid for the option

   See Section 3.2 of your Study Text

15. **B** The writer of an option always has a potential obligation. The holder of an option has a right, but not an obligation

   See Section 3.3.4 of your Study Text

16. **A** The writer faces potentially unlimited losses

   See Section 3.2 of your Study Text

17. **B** Only buyers of options must pay the premium

   See Section 3.2 of your Study Text

4. Financial Products

Questions

1. ✗ Richard raises a mortgage of £24,000 from a friend. The loan is interest-free and will be repaid at £400 per month. Richard wishes to ensure that his friend is repaid in the event of his own death. What type of life assurance policy would be the most relevant and cost-effective for Richard?

    A Decreasing term

    B Increasing term

    C Endowment

    D Whole of life

2. ✗ Simon wishes to provide £50,000 for his dependants in the event of his death. Which type of life assurance policy would be the least expensive to achieve this objective?

    A Term assurance

    B Whole life assurance

    C Endowment

    D Family income benefit

3. ✓ A company pension scheme under which participants receive a pension on retirement based on their final salary is called a

    A Deferred benefits scheme

    B Defined benefits scheme

    C Deferred contribution scheme

    D Defined contribution scheme

4. ✓ Which of the following is not a common characteristic of the property market?

    A Heterogeneous

    B Indivisible

    C Liquid

    D Decentralised

5. ✓ A small self-administered scheme can have no more than

    A 8 members

    B 11 members

    C 13 members

    D 16 members

6. Which of the following is not one of the features of offshore investment bonds?

    A The underlying life funds suffer little or no tax

    B Charges are low, making offshore bonds especially appropriate for a short-term holding period

    C Withdrawals of up to 5% of the original investment may be taken for 20 years without an immediate tax liability

    D Offices issuing the bonds may be situated in locations that include the Channel Islands, Isle of Man, Dublin and Luxembourg

7. Assuming the same interest rates, which types of mortgage will have the lowest total of interest payments over a 25-year duration?

    A Low-cost endowment mortgage

    B Pension-linked mortgage

    C Repayment mortgage

    D ISA-linked mortgage

8. What is the rule with respect to maximum charges applied by managers for new stakeholder pension plans?

    A 1.5% for the first 10 years; 1.0% thereafter

    B 1.5% for the first 5 years; 1.0% thereafter

    C 1% for the first 10 years; 0.5% thereafter

    D 1% for the first 5 years; 0.5% thereafter

9. What is meant by 'the life assured' in respect of a life policy?

    A The person who pays the premiums

    B The person who benefits from the policy

    C The person whose death will lead to the policy paying out

    D None of the above

10. Which best describes term assurance?

    A Cover against loss of earnings over a defined number of years

    B Any life policy with a surrender value

    C A ten-year savings-linked policy

    D Cover against the possibility of death during a specified period

11. Do term assurance policies have a surrender value?

    A Yes, in all cases

    B No, in all cases

    C No, except in the case of level term policies

    D Yes, but only in the first 14 days

12. ✗ **In what ways are pensions tax-efficient?**

      I   Pension contributions are generally tax-deductible

      II   Pension payments out are generally tax-deductible

      III   Pension funds do not generally pay tax

      IV   Pension payments are taxed at 17½%

(A) I, II and III

B II and IV

C I and III

D I and IV

13. ✓ **What is the tax treatment in respect of receipt of pension payments?**

A Tax-free in respect of both lump sum and pension

B Lump sum and pension are both taxable

C Only the lump sum element is taxed

(D) Only the annual payment is taxed

14. ✗ **Which of the following incurs the lowest overall interest?**

A Endowment

B Low cost endowment

(C) Deferred interest

D Repayment mortgage

15. ✓ **What is the upper age limit for becoming a member of a registered pension scheme?**

A 70 years

(B) 75 years

C 77 years

D 80 years

16. ✓ **Brian would like to invest 'indirectly' in property. Which one of the following would not be a means to do this?**

A Property bonds

B Property company shares which are listed on the Stock Exchange

(C) Building Society ISA

D Property unit trusts

17. ✗ **For a defined benefits occupational scheme**

A The benefits must go up with RPI

B The benefits must go up with an average earnings index

C The benefits are based on average earnings close to retirement

(D) The benefits rise with average earnings over working life

18. How much of one's pension pot can be taken as a tax-free lump sum?

A 15%

B 20%

C 25%

D Nil

19. Which of the following is a feature of a unit-linked life contract, which is being considered by an investor as a regular savings plan?

A No surrender penalty on encashment

B Tax free if term is for more than ten years, or ¾ term if less

C Tax relief for insurance element of payments

D Cheapest form of life assurance

20. What does 'AER' stand for?

A Annual Equivalent Rate

B Exponential Average Rate

C Extra Accrued Rights

D Endowment Annual Return

21. What is the lifetime allowance for pension benefits in 2010/11?

A £1,400,000

B £1,650,000

C £1,750,000

D £1,800,000

22. What is the annual allowance contribution limit tor pension plans in 2010/11?

A £225,000

B £235,000

C £245,000

D £255,000

23. In the event of death during the term, how much of the fund value will an investment bond typically pay?

A 80%

B 100%

C 101%

D 105%

24. ✓ **What rate will a higher rate taxpayer pay on capital gains from an investment bond?**

   A 10%

   B 18%

   Ⓒ 20%

   D 0%

25. ✓ **A woman earned £12,000 in the current fiscal year. She received interest of £1,000 per month from a building society. At what rate is this taxed?**

   A 18%

   Ⓑ 20%

   C 32½%

   D 40%

26. ✓ **Which of the following can term assurance not be used for?**

   A To protect the amount outstanding on a repayment mortgage

   B To provide a lump sum on death

   C To protect a spouse against the death of the policyholder, whenever this should occur

   Ⓓ To protect any children until they are 18

27. ✓ **An investor deposits £10,000 into an interest-bearing account for three years. If the simple interest convention is paid annually at a rate of 4.5%, how much net interest will the investor have earned in the three-year period?**

   A £450

   Ⓑ £1,080

   C £1,215

   D £1,350

28. ✓ **Which of the following does not describe a type of term life assurance?**

   Ⓐ With profits

   B Decreasing

   C Level

   D Increasing

29. ✓ **What is the maximum percentage of a client's personal pension fund that normally can be taken as tax-free cash?**

   A 15%

   B 20%

   Ⓒ 25%

   D 30%

30. ✓ **With regard to State pensions, which of the following is false?**

Ⓐ Anyone paying National Insurance contributions for 20 years and reaching State Pension age after 5 April 2010 will receive 75% of the full State pension

B Anyone paying National Insurance contributions for 30 years and reaching State Pension age after 5 April 2010 will receive a full State pension

C Pension payments are made gross, but are taxable

D The current ages of retirement are 65 for men and 60 for women

31. ✓ **What would you expect the interest rate on a secured loan to be, compared with an unsecured loan for the same amount and for the same borrower?**

A Higher

B The same

Ⓒ Lower

D Impossible to say

32. ✓ **Which of the following types of mortgage is not correctly described as an interest-only mortgage?**

A Endowment

B Pension

C ISA

Ⓓ Repayment

33. ✓ **A life policy is a contract between which of the following?**

A Underwriter and investment manager

B Individual and investment manager

Ⓒ Individual and insurance company

D Investment manager and insurance company

34. ✗ **If you have a pension-linked mortgage, how much of the final fund will normally be available to repay the loan?**

A 25%

B 33.3%

Ⓒ 20%

D 35%

35. ✗ **An occupational money purchase scheme can be described as**

A Defined contributions

Ⓑ Defined benefits

C Additional voluntary contributions

D Contributory scheme

36. ✓ Mr Wong is a 40% rate taxpayer who lives in the UK. He deposits £10,000 in a building society together with a completed R85. How should he be taxed on his earned interest?

   A Nil at source, 40% via his tax return

   B 20% at source, 20% via his tax return

   C 40% at source

   D None of the above

37. ✓ A bank advertises a loan at 12% per annum, with interest charged quarterly. What is the effective annual rate?

   A 12%

   B 12.55%

   C 16.99%

   D 12.3%

38. ✓ A credit card company is quoting an annual interest rate of 18%, charged monthly. What is the annual effective rate?

   A 18.5%

   B 19.25%

   C 19.56%

   D 20.5%

39. ✦ A borrower is quoted an interest rate of 8%, charged quarterly. What is the annual effective rate (AER)?

   A 8.00%

   B 8.24%

   C 8.50%

   D 9.24%

40. ✓ A borrower is quoted an interest rate of 12%, charged semi-annually. What is the annual effective rate (AER)?

   A 11.36%

   B 13.36%

   C 12.36%

   D 14.36%

41. ✓ **A borrower is quoted an interest rate of 9%, charged semi-annually. What is the annual effective rate (AER)?**

    A 8.20%

    Ⓑ 9.20%

    C 10.20%

    D 11.20%

---

42. ✓ **A borrower is quoted an interest rate of 10%, charged quarterly. What is the annual effective rate (AER)?**

    Ⓐ 10.40%

    B 9.40%

    C 11.40%

    D 10.00%

Answers

1.   **A**   The capital outstanding is decreasing by £400 per month, so a decreasing term policy would be the cheapest and most relevant type of insurance for Richard to take out on his life

     See Section 7 of your Study Text

2.   **A**   Term assurance would be the cheapest, as this is designed to provide a lump sum and has no Investment content. Family income benefit would not be suitable for this purpose, as the sum assured decreases during the term of the cover but provides a constant annual benefit

     See Section 7 of your Study Text

3.   **B**   An alternative name for a final salary type scheme is a defined benefit scheme

     See Section 3.3.1 of your Study Text

4.   **C**   It might take sometime to sell a property so it is normally described as being an illiquid market

     See Section 2.1 of your Study Text

5.   **B**

     See Section 3.4.2 of your Study Text

6.   **B**   Charges are relatively high and would typically involve a substantial sacrifice of capital if the holding period is only short.

     See Section 4.2 of your Study Text

7.   **C**   A, B and D will have higher monthly outlay and interest payments than C because they are all interest-only type mortgages. With a repayment mortgage, the capital is being repaid and so the interest charged will be decreasing over the term of the mortgage

     See Section 6 of your Study Text

8.   **A**   For new plans, charges are limited to 1.5% of the fund value pa for the first ten years and 1% pa thereafter. For plans started before April 2005, a limit of 1% applies in all years

     See Section 3.5 of your Study Text

9.   **C**   The life assured is the person whose death will lead to the payout on the policy

     See Section 7 of your Study Text

10.   **D**   Term assurance is a contract with an insurer which covers the risk of death over a specified term. There is no surrender value in the contract

     See Section 7 of your Study Text

11.   **B**   There is no surrender value with term assurance

     See Section 7 of your Study Text

12. **C** Pension contributions within annual allowances are tax-deductible for employee and employer. Pension funds do not generally pay tax. Although the tax credit on UK dividends has been lost, there are no other taxes due

See Section 3.7 of your Study Text

13. **D** The pension payment is taxed as earned income

See Section 3.7 of your Study Text

14. **D** Repayment mortgages have the lowest overall level of interest, as capital is being repaid over the term of the mortgage, so the level of interest decreases as capital is repaid

See Section 6 of your Study Text

15. **B**

See Section 3.8 of your Study Text

16. **C** A Building Society ISA is not an indirect property investment

See Section 2.1 of your Study Text

17. **C** Defined benefits schemes are also known as final salary schemes, so it makes sense that the benefits are based on remuneration close to retirement and service with the employer

See Section 3.3.1 of your Study Text

18. **C** 25% may be taken as a tax-free lump sum

See Section 3.4 of your Study Text

19. **B** The policy will be a qualifying investment after ten years and will therefore give a tax-free return in the hands of the investor

See Section 7 of your Study Text

20. **A** EAR stands for annual equivalent annual rate. This may alternatively might be referred to as the annual equivalent rate

See Section 5.2 of your Study Text

21. **D** The lifetime allowance is proposed to be £1,800,000 for the years 2010/11 to 2015/16.

See Section 3.6 of your Study Text

22. **D** The annual allowance is proposed to be £255,000 for the years 2010/11 to 2015/16.

See Section 3.6 of your Study Text

23. **C**

See Section 4.1 of your Study Text

24. **D** The fund will generally have paid tax at 20% on income. Accordingly, a higher rate taxpayer will have nothing further to pay since capital gains tax is charged at 18%

See Section 4.1 of your Study Text

25. **B** Investment income from a building society would be taxed at 20% for an investor who is a basic rate taxpayer

See Section 1 of your Study Text

26. **C** It will only protect against death for the term specified in the policy

See Section 7 of your Study Text

27. **B** Remember that the withholding tax on interest is 20%

£10,000 × 4.5% = £450 per year earned in interest. Thus, over three years, the investor earns £1,350.

Now to adjust for tax: £1,350 × (1 − Tax rate) = £1,080

See Section 1 of your Study Text

28. **A** With profits relates to whole of life and endowment policies

See Section 7 of your Study Text

29. **C** 25% of the fund may be taken as tax-free cash

See Section 3.7 of your Study Text

30. **A** In order to receive the full State pension, the individual retiring after 5 April 2010 must have credits for 30 qualifying years. Those with fewer qualifying years will receive one thirtieth of the full amount for each qualifying year

See Section 3.2 of your Study Text

31. **C** All other things being equal, this is true

See Section 5.3 of your Study Text

32. **D** A repayment mortgage (sometimes known as capital and interest mortgage) is not a type of interest-only mortgage

See Section 6.1 of your Study Text

33. **C**

See Section 7 of your Study Text

34. **A** The tax-free cash part of the fund can be used to repay the mortgage

See Section 6.2 of your Study Text

35. **A** Defined contribution schemes are money purchase arrangements. 'Defined Benefit scheme' is another name for a final salary scheme

See Section 3.3.2 of your Study Text

36. **B** Despite the fact that he has completed an R85, the building society should not pay the interest gross since Mr Wong, as a higher rate taxpayer, is not entitled

See Section 1 of your Study Text

37. **B** If interest is quoted at 12% p.a., charged on a quarterly basis then the effective annual rate is calculated as follows

$$\frac{12\% \text{ per annum}}{4 \text{ quarters}} = 3\% \text{ each quarter}$$

Therefore
$$(1+r_1) \times (1+r_2) \times (1+r_3) \times (1+r_4) = 1 + AER$$

$$AER = [1.03 \times 1.03 \times 1.03 \times 1.03] - 1$$
$$= 1.1255 - 1$$
$$= 0.1255 = 12.55\%$$

See Section 5.2 of your Study Text

38. **C** If interest is quoted at 18% p.a., but charged monthly, then the AER is calculated as follows.

$$\frac{18\% \text{ per annum}}{12 \text{ months}} = 1.5\% \text{ each month}$$

Therefore
$$(1+r_1) \times (1+r_2) \times (1+r_3) \times (1+r_4) \times (1+r_5) \times (1+r_6) \times (1+r_7) \times (1+r_8) \times (1+r_9) \times (1+r_{10}) \times (1+r_{11}) \times (1+r_{12}) = 1 + AER$$

$$= (1+r)^{12} = 1 + AER$$

$$AER = (1+0.015)^{12} - 1$$
$$= 1.1956 - 1$$
$$= 0.1956 = 19.56\%$$

See Section 5.2 of your Study Text

39. **B** One way to calculate this is to take a loan of £100. At a quoted interest rate of 8% per annum, quarterly rate interest of 2% on £100 is paid at the end of quarter 1, i.e. £2. The next quarter interest of 2% is paid on £102, i.e. £2.04. In quarter 3, interest of 2% is paid on £104.04, i.e. £2.08. In quarter 4, interest of 2% is paid on £106.12, i.e. £2.12. Adding up the interest paid through the year gives £8.24. Therefore the effective rate is 8.24%.

Another way to calculate this is as follows.

8% interest per annum / 4 quarters = 2% per quarter

Therefore, $(1+r_1) \times (1+r_2) \times (1+r_3) \times (1+r_4) = 1 + AER$

Thus, $AER = \{(1 + 0.02) \times (1 + 0.02) \times (1 + 0.02) \times (1 + 0.02)\} - 1$

$$= (1.02 \times 1.02 \times 1.02 \times 1.02) - 1$$

$$= 1.0824 - 1$$

$$= 0.0824 = 8.24\%$$

See Section 5.2 of your Study Text

40.   **C**   We can to take a loan of £1,000. At a quoted interest rate of 12% per annum, semi-annual interest of 6% on £1,000 is paid at the end of the first six months, i.e. £60. The second six-months interest of 6% is paid on £1,060, i.e. £63.60.

Adding up the interest paid through the year gives £123.60. Therefore the effective rate is 12.36%.

Another way to calculate this is as follows.

12% interest per annum / 2 semi-annual periods = 6% per six-months

Therefore, $(1+r_1) \times (1+r_2) = 1 + \text{AER}$

$$\begin{aligned} \text{Thus, AER} &= \{(1 + 0.06) \times (1 + 0.06)\} - 1 \\ &= (1.06 \times 1.06) - 1 \\ &= 1.1236 - 1 \\ &= 0.1236 = 12.36\% \end{aligned}$$

See Section 5.2 of your Study Text

41.   **B**   Consider a loan of £100. At a quoted interest rate of 9% per annum, semi-annual interest of 4.5% on £100 is paid at the end of the first six months, i.e. £4.50. The second six months interest of 4.5% is paid on £104.50, i.e. £4.70.

Adding up the interest paid through the year gives £9.20. Therefore the effective rate is 9.20%.

Another way to calculate this is as follows.

9% interest per annum/2 semi-annual periods = 4.5% per six-months

Therefore, $(1+r_1) \times (1+r_2) = 1 + \text{AER}$

$$\begin{aligned} \text{Thus, AER} &= \{(1 + 0.045) \times (1 + 0.045)\} - 1 \\ &= (1.045 \times 1.045) - 1 \\ &= 1.0920 - 1 \\ &= 0.0920 = 9.20\% \end{aligned}$$

See Section 5.2 of your Study Text

42.   **A**   Suppose there is a loan of £1,000. At a quoted interest rate of 10% per annum, quarterly rate interest of 2.5% on £1,000 is paid at the end of quarter 1, i.e. £25. The next quarter interest of 2.5% is paid on £1,025, i.e. £25.63. In quarter 3, interest of 2.5% is paid on £1,050.63, i.e. £26.26. In quarter 4, interest of 2.5% is paid on £1,076.89, i.e. £26.92. Adding up the interest paid through the year gives £103.81. Therefore the effective rate is 10.40%.

Another way to calculate this is as follows.

10% interest per annum / 4 quarters = 2.5% per quarter

Therefore, $(1+r_1) \times (1+r_2) \times (1+r_3) \times (1+r_4) = 1 + \text{AER}$

$$\begin{aligned} \text{Thus, AER} &= \{(1 + 0.025) \times (1 + 0.025) \times (1 + 0.025) \times (1 + 0.025)\} - 1 \\ &= (1.025 \times 1.025 \times 1.025 \times 1.025) - 1 \\ &= 1.104 - 1 \\ &= 0.104 = 10.4\% \end{aligned}$$

See Section 5.2 of your Study Text

5. Pooled Investment Funds

Questions

1. Which two of the following are roles of the unit trust manager?

      I   Making investment decisions

      II   Buying and selling investments for the fund

      III   Auditing the fund

      IV   Safeguarding the fund's assets

A   I and III

B   II and IV

C   I and IV

D   I and II

2. Which of the following best describes a type of unit trust?

A   A savings plan referred to as a unit trust, which relies on stock market growth and dividends to achieve capital gains for investors

B   A means of life assurance referred to as a unit trust, which involves investing in the stock market with certain tax advantages if the unit investments are held for a specified period of time

C   A listed company referred to as a unit trust, which relies on stock market growth and dividends to achieve capital gains

D   A fund referred to as a unit trust, which relies on stock market growth and dividends to achieve capital gains for investors

3. What is the main motivation behind the creation of UCITS?

A   To allow fund managers to charge more than a 15% spread

B   To allow a unit trust to be marketed throughout Europe

C   To allow geared futures and options funds to be freely marketed to the British public

D   To allow any gains made within the fund to remain tax-free

4. Which of the following best describes an OEIC?

A   A company in which clients invest

B   A trust in which clients invest

C   A company specially set up, so it can continually issue and redeem its shares, in which clients invest

D   A company in which clients invest, which always delivers income and capital gains tax free

5. ✓ **Which one of the following investments will often trade at a discount?**

   A   ISAs

   Ⓑ   Investment trust shares

   C   Units in a unit trust

   D   Shares in a listed company

6. ✓ **A Qualified Investor Scheme**

   Ⓐ   Needs FSA approval to become a non-UCITS retail scheme

   B   Is a scheme that may be marketed to the general public in the UK

   C   Is an approved investment trust regular savings plan

   D   Cannot convert to become a UCITS scheme

7. ✗ **Which one of the following statements is false?**

   A   The fund manager for a unit trust must invest in accordance with the criteria laid out in the Trust Deed

   B   Investing in a unit trust often allows private investors to gain greater diversification

   Ⓒ   Tracker funds are passively managed funds

   D   All unit trusts will have broadly similar returns on investment

8. ✗ **The price of an investment trust's shares represents**

   A   The market price based on supply and demand

   B   The discount available

   Ⓒ   The net asset value

   D   The value of the underlying investments

9. ✗ **If a unit trust manager quotes on an offer basis, he wants to**

   Ⓐ   Create more units

   B   Sell new units on creation

   C   Encourage investors to sell to the manager

   D   Offer a dividend

10. ✗ **When an investment trust share is at a large discount to NAV, which of the following is true?**

   A   Future capital growth could be higher than with a direct investment

   B   There is a guaranteed level of capital growth

   C   There will be no capital growth

   Ⓓ   Capital gain is achieved at the expense of income

11. × **Which of the following aspects regarding investment trusts are true?**

       I   Their capital structure is fixed

       II   They are traded on the Stock Exchange

       III   They are all companies

       IV   They can borrow as long as it is permitted in their constitutional documents

    A   I, II, III and IV

    D   I, III and IV

    C   II and III

    D   I, II and III

12. » **Who is the legal owner of assets in an OEIC?**

    A   Trustee

    B   Authorised Corporate Director

    C   Manager

    D   Depository

13. ✓ **An investment trust is**

    A   A closed-ended fund public limited company

    B   An open-ended fund with a trust deed

    C   A closed-ended fund in which extra units can be issued

    D   An open-ended fund in which extra units can be issued

14. ✓ **Which of the following best describes an 'OEIC'?**

    A   The French equivalent term for a UCITS

    B   An Operational Equity Investment Corporation

    C   An open-ended company with variable capital

    D   A company mainly investing in European securities

15. ✓ **What are trustees of a unit trust not responsible for?**

    A   Marketing the units

    B   Maintaining a register

    C   Ensuring the manager obeys the trust deed

    D   Setting up the scheme

16. × **What is the 'NAV' of a share?**

    A   Notional asset value ÷ Share price

    B   (Assets minus liabilities) ÷ Number of shares

    C   Market capitalisation ÷ Number of shares

    D   Assets ÷ Share price

17. At what price does a unit trust sell units to investors?

    A   Bid

    B   Offer

    C   Mid

    D   Creation

18. Why would a unit trust manager price on a bid basis?

    I   Encourage sellers

    II   Discourage sellers

    III   Encourage buyers

    IV   Discourage buyers

    A   I and IV

    B   II and III

    C   I and II

    D   III and IV

19. Which of the following is true of investment trust companies?

    I   They must be UK resident

    II   They must distribute at least 90% of their income

    III   The Board of Directors can change the investment manager

    IV   Income must be derived from shares or securities

    A   I, II, III and IV

    B   I, II and III

    C   I, III and IV

    D   III and IV

20. An investment trust share price is 40p, whilst the NAV 36p. There is a

    A   Premium of 11.1%

    B   Discount of 11.1%

    C   Premium of 10.0%

    D   Discount of 10.0%

21. Which of the following is false in respect of Real Estate Investment Trusts (REITs)?

    A   No one person can hold more than 10% of the shares

    B   95% of taxable profits must be distributed to investors

    C   The REIT withholds basic rate tax on distributed profits

    D   The REIT must be listed on a Recognised Investment Exchange

22. ✗ **Which of the following statements is true?**

Ⓐ Investment trusts are legal trusts set up with the sole purpose of investing in the securities of other companies

B The price of investment trust shares are determined by taking the net asset value of the trust and dividing by the number of shares in issue

C Where investment trust shares trade at a discount to asset value, there may be a takeover launched for those shares

D Investment trusts are a particular type of unit trust

---

23. ✓ **Which of the following is not a feature of Exchange-Traded Funds (ETFs)?**

A No Stamp Duty Reserve Tax is payable by the purchaser

Ⓑ The funds are managed with an active investment strategy

C A price quote will be available throughout the trading day

D ETFs are open-ended funds

Answers

1.   **D**   Statement III is the role of the auditor and Statement IV is the role of the trustee. Statement II is a bit of a grey area. Although officially it is the responsibility of the trustee, he will often delegate this to the manager. Of the choices available, I and II are best.

   See Section 2.1 of your Study Text

2.   **D**   Answer B describes an endowment policy and answer C describes an investment trust. D is a better answer than A because you can just make a one-off contribution to a unit trust. It does not have to be part of a regular savings plan

   See Section 2.1 of your Study Text

3.   **B**   UCITS status is not automatic: application must be made to the FSA

   See Section 2.9 of your Study Text

4.   **C**   An OEIC is a type of ICVC (Investment Company with Variable Capital), which can change its capital structure over time

   See Section 3.1 of your Study Text

5.   **B**   The discount arises because investors access the various companies in which the investment trust (IT) invests only indirectly and/or because the quality of management of the IT is relatively weak

   See Section 4.2 of your Study Text

6.   **A**   A QIS is a fund that can only be marketed to professional investors, and can convert to become a UCITS scheme if it meets the UCITS conditions

   See Section 2.3 of your Study Text

7.   **D**   Tracker funds are not actively managed (hence 'passively' managed), because they only invest in all the shares in an index, e.g. FTSE 100. The risks of a unit trust will vary in line with the investment objectives

   See Section 2 of your Study Text

8.   **A**   The price of an investment trust is the market price and is determined by the supply and demand of the shares in question

   See Section 4.2 of your Study Text

9.   **C**   Offer basis is pricing around the highest possible price and this means that there is high demand for the units

   See Section 2.6 of your Study Text

10.   **A**   The discount will mean that each share will have a potential capital gain, for example if the discount narrows or the trust winds up, because the share is currently priced at less than the assets it represents

   See Section 4.2 of your Study Text

11. **A** If you got this wrong, then go back to your study material notes and re-read the section on investment trusts

See Section 4.1 of your Study Text

12. **D** The Depositary acts as legal owner and safeguard of assets in an OEIC. The Authorised Corporate Director manages the investments, trades the securities and prices the shares in the OEIC at net asset value

See Section 3.2 of your Study Text

13. **A** ITs are closed-ended companies quoted on the London Stock Exchange as public limited companies

See Section 4.1 of your Study Text

14. **C** It is an investment company with variable capital

See Section 3.1 of your Study Text

15. **A** The managers of the unit trust are responsible for the marketing of the fund

See Section 2.1 of your Study Text

16. **B** NAV is the value of assets per share after deducting the liabilities of the company

See Section 4.2 of your Study Text

17. **B** The unit trust sells the units at the offer price, which is the higher price. (The bid price is lower)

See Section 2.5 of your Study Text

18. **B** Bid price is the lowest price at which the unit trust can be sold. This is to discourage people from selling and to make the trust more attractive to buyers

See Section 2.6 of your Study Text

19. **C**

See Section 4.1 of your Study Text

20. **A** The share is at a premium because it is priced above the net asset value of the holding of the trust. $4p \div 36p \times 100 = 11.1\%$

See Section 4.2 of your Study Text

21. **B** A REIT must distribute a minimum of 90% of profits from letting

See Section 7.2 of your Study Text

22. **C** Investment trusts are companies, not legal trusts or unit trusts. Their price is determined by supply and demand for that share. Investment trust shares do tend to trade at a discount to their net asset value

See Section 4.1 of your Study Text

23. **B** ETFs track indices and, as passive tracker-style funds, they are relatively low cost.

See Section 5 of your Study Text

6. Investment Wrappers

Questions

1. ✓ **An ISA can be described as**

   Ⓐ A tax-efficient savings scheme

   B A collective investment scheme

   C A company investing in another company

   D A personal pension plan

2. ✓ **Which one of the following statements is true with regard to ISAs, in respect of 2010/11?**

   A The maximum that an investor aged 58 can invest in a cash ISA is £7,200

   Ⓑ Income and capital gains are tax-free

   C The maximum overall investment for a person aged 60 is £14,400

   D An investor cannot open both a stocks and shares ISA and a cash ISA with different providers in the same tax year

3. ✓ **Which of the following patterns of transactions is not possible within ISA rules, in a newly opened cash ISA, if all transactions occur in the current tax year?**

   A £1,000 deposit; £1,000 withdrawal; £2,000 deposit

   B £1,500 deposit; £800 withdrawal; £500 withdrawal; £2,000 deposit

   C £1,000 deposit; £2,500 deposit; £200 withdrawal

   Ⓓ £4,000 deposit; £3,000 withdrawal; £3,000 deposit

4. ✓ **What is the maximum payable into a cash ISA by Mr Chakravarti, aged 34, in the current tax year?**

   A £1,800

   Ⓑ £5,100

   C £3,600

   D £7,200

5. ✗ **Which of the following is true of a stocks and shares ISA?**

   A Cannot be held by anyone under 18 years

   B Can invest in as many ISAs as you like

   Ⓒ Will perform better than other investments which are taxed

   D Can invest any amount of money in an ISA

6. How much can a married couple invest in total in ISAs in the fiscal year 2010/11?

   A £10,000

   B £7,200

   C £10,200

   D £20,400

7. Of the following dates, which indicate a time period within which two stocks and shares ISAs could be started?

   A 6 April 2010 and 6 December 2010

   B 1 April 2010 and 5 March 2011

   C 30 June 2010 and 31 January 2011

   D 31 December 2010 and 5 April 2011

8. If a 45-year old invests £1,500 into the cash component of an ISA in the tax year 2010/11, what is the maximum stocks and shares investment she can make into the ISA in the same year?

   A £10,200

   B £8,700

   C £7,200

   D £5,700

9. For a 55-year old investor, the maximum investment in a stocks and shares ISA in the fiscal year 2010/11 is

   A £10,200

   B £7,200

   C £6,400

   D £3,600

10. The cash component of an ISA is permitted to hold stakeholder products that guarantee a return of the capital invested of at least

   A 100%

   B 99%

   C 98%

   D 95%

11. Which of the following is not a characteristic of a Child Trust Fund (CTF)?

   A All income within the CTF is free of tax

   B A maximum contribution of £3,000 each year can be invested in the fund

   C The child has access to the funds at the age of 18

   D All capital gains within the CTF are free of tax

12. ✓ **The age at which a child takes complete control of a Child Trust Fund is**

    A 14

    B 16

    Ⓒ 18

    D 21

---

13. ⁎ **Which of the following is not correct regarding ISA transfers?**

    A The investor can transfer part or all of their cash ISAs from previous tax years into stocks and shares ISAs, with their present or another provider, without affecting their current annual ISA investment allowance

    B The investor can transfer all (but not only part of) the money saved so far in a current tax year cash ISA into a stocks and shares ISA, with their present or another provider

    C After the first year, the investor may transfer an ISA to a different manager, in which case all assets and financial instruments in the ISA must be transferred

    Ⓓ ISA managers are required to allow transfers between managers, although a manager is not required to accept a transfer in

Answers

1. **A**   Both income and capital gains are tax exempt within an ISA

    See Section 1.1 of your Study Text

2. **B**   The maximum investment (2010/11) is £10,200, of which £5,100 may be invested in a cash ISA

    See Section 1.2 of your Study Text

3. **D**   Under choice A, a total of £3,000 has been deposited. For B, £3,500 has been deposited. Under choice C, £3,500 has been deposited. Choice D breaks the rules as it involves a total of £7,000 in deposits in the same tax year

    See Section 1.2 of your Study Text

4. **B**   £5,100 may be paid into a cash ISA in the tax year 2010/11

    See Section 1.2 of your Study Text

5. **A**   It is not possible for anyone under 18 to purchase an ISA. (Over 16s can open and contribute to the cash component of an ISA)

    See Section 1.1 of your Study Text

6. **D**   The annual limit for ISAs is £10,200 per person. Therefore the total they can invest would be £20,400

    See Section 1.2 of your Study Text

7. **B**   These dates span two tax years, so two stocks and shares ISAs may be started

    See Section 1.1 of your Study Text

8. **B**   £10,200 – £1,500. This would leave £8,700 for investment in the stocks and shares component of the ISA

    See Section 1.2 of your Study Text

9. **A**   The maximum investment in a stocks and shares ISA is £10,200 for the fiscal 2010/11

    See Section 1.2 of your Study Text

10. **D**   This is referred to as the '5% test'

    See Section 1.2 of your Study Text

11. **B**   Child Trust Funds (CTFs) represent an incentive for families to save for the long-term. These are long-term savings and investment accounts, with all income and capital gains free of tax. The Government has awarded each eligible child a voucher, worth £250, to start investing in the CTF, with a maximum contribution of £1,200 each year. The child then has access to the CTF when they reach the age of 18

    See Section 2 of your Study Text

12. **C**   The child takes control of the fund at the age of 18 and may spend it as they wish. At age 16, the child can make active decisions on how the money is managed

    See Section 2 of your Study Text

13.   **C**   C being incorrect, the true position is as follows. The investor may transfer an ISA to a different manager in the year of subscription, in which case the entire ISA subscription for that year must be transferred. After the first year however, partial (or full) transfers between ISA managers are permitted.

See Section 1.3 of your Study Text

7. Financial Services Regulation

Questions

1. Which one of the following is a change that has not been implemented by the Government in respect of the economy and financial services regulation?

   A The absorption of the then existing regulatory bodies in to one single body, namely the FSA

   B The transfer of the management of interest rates to a new committee headed by the Bank of England

   C The publication of a new Financial Services and Markets Act

   D The transfer of banking supervision to the Bank of England

2. According to the Data Protection Act 1998, with whom must persons processing personal data register?

   A FSA

   B HMT

   C Competition Commissioner

   D Information Commissioner

3. Which one of the following statements is false?

   A Treating customers fairly reinforces Principle 6 of the FSA's Principles for Business

   B The FSMT can consider new evidence that has come to light since an initial decision was made

   C The European Commission implements EU policy such as the Capital Requirements Directive

   D If a firm has breached a rule of the FSA then a private person can use s71 of FSMA to sue the firm

4. Which one of the following is not a sanction with respect to data protection regulation?

   A A jail term of two years

   B A £5,000 fine in the Magistrates' Court

   C An Enforcement Notice issued by the Information Commissioner

   D An unlimited fine in the Crown Court

5. Which of the following is not part of the FSA's statutory objectives?

   A Maintaining confidence in the UK financial system

   B Consumer protection

   C Promoting the competence of investment advisers

   D Reduction in financial crime

6. Which of the following is true of regulation of financial services in the UK?

   A Primary legislation is found in FSMA 2000

   B Primary legislation is found in the UCITS directive

   C The FSA was responsible for drafting primary legislation

   D Financial services in the UK are self-regulating

7. Which of the following is not a grouping of controlled functions for approved persons?

   A Governing functions

   B Necessary functions

   C Systems and control functions

   D Customer functions

8. The three stages of money laundering are

   A Placement, layering and integration

   B Placement, churning and integration

   C Switching, layering and assimilation

   D Switching, churning and assimilation

9. Which of the following best describes market abuse?

   A A criminal offence

   B A breach of contract

   C A civil offence

   D None of the above

10. Under the Money Laundering Regulations 2007, authorised firms are responsible for

        I   Checking the identity of customers

        II   Checking the source of funds

        III Reporting suspicious customers to the authorities

        IV Assisting in the arrest of suspects

   A I and II

   B I, II and III

   C I, III and IV

   D II, III and IV

11. A private investor may make a claim under the Financial Services Compensation Scheme if he loses money as a result of

      I   A fraud committed by an authorised person

      II   A breach of rules by an authorised person

      III   The liquidation of an authorised person

  A I only

  B I and II

  C I and III

  D III only

12. Which of the following is a means of obtaining authorisation to conduct investment business in the UK?

  A Application to the FSA

  B Application to the SEC

  C Membership of an RIE

  D Application to ICMA

13. Which of the following is responsible for drafting legislation concerning investment protection in the UK?

  A Financial Services Authority

  B Department for Business, Innovation and Skills

  C Her Majesty's Treasury

  D Office of Fair Trading

14. Which of the following is responsible for insider dealing legislation?

  A FSA

  B BIS

  C HMT

  D LSE

15. Which best describes 'layering' in the context of money laundering?

  A Buying units in an unregulated fund

  B Disguising the source of money

  C Purchasing derivative financial instruments

  D Making many different payments

16. Select the statement below which most appropriately describes the style of regulation introduced by the Financial Services and Markets Act 2000.

  A Self-regulation

  B Regulation by the consumer

  C Ombudsman regulated

  D Statutory regulation

17. Suspected money laundering transactions should usually be reported to the

  A Bank of England

  B Serious Fraud Office

  C Stock Exchange

  D Serious Organised Crime Agency

18. Which body can remove approval from an approved person?

  A Office of Fair Trading

  B Treasury

  C Department for Business, Innovation and Skills

  D Financial Services Authority

19. If an individual has a total claim of £35,000 for investments, what would be the maximum amount of compensation he could receive under the Financial Services Compensation Scheme?

  A Nil

  B £34,500

  C £35,000

  D £48,000

20. In what circumstances does the Financial Services Compensation Scheme pay out?

  A When a firm closes down and an investor loses money

  B When poor advice is given and an investor loses money

  C When the FSA does not regulate efficiently and an investor loses money

  D When any investor loses money

21. For protected investments, the Financial Services Compensation Scheme sets a maximum payout of

  A £20,000 plus 90% of next £20,000

  B £30,000 plus 90% of next £20,000

  C £30,000 plus 90% of next £30,000

  D £50,000

22. The market abuse legislation does not cover trading on

   A LSE

   Ⓑ PLUS

   C LIFFE

   D NYSE

23. Regarding complaints procedures, which of the following need to be in place?

   I   Written procedures to handle complaints

   II   Advice to the client where to go if not satisfied

   III A complaints officer

   IV   Review of all complaints by the regulator

   Ⓐ I, II, III and IV

   B I, II and III

   C I and II

   D I, III and IV

24. Which statements are true regarding insider dealing legislation in the Criminal Justice Act 1993?

   I   Offences may only be committed by an individual, not a company

   II   Encouraging a third party to deal on the basis of insider information is an offence

   III UK equities, gilts and related derivatives are all caught by the legislation

   IV   Disclosure of price-sensitive information to a third party (other than the normal course of employment) is an offence

   A I, II and III

   B I, II and IV

   C II, III and IV

   Ⓓ I, II, III and IV

25. If a complaint investigated by a firm has not been conciliated, to which of the following can the complaint be referred?

   A Financial Services and Markets Tribunal

   Ⓑ Financial Ombudsman Service

   C Complaints Commissioner

   D Financial Services Compensation Scheme

26. The Financial Ombudsman Service was set up by

   A The FSA

   B The Bank of England

   Ⓒ HMT

   D The Lord Chancellor

27. Which one of the following statements about the Financial Ombudsman Service is false?

A   The maximum award by the Ombudsman is £100,000 plus costs

B   There is a registration fee and appeals process

C   It can hear cases regarding non-regulated activities as part of its voluntary jurisdiction

D   It is available to all clients

28. If the outcome of the Financial Ombudsman investigation is declined by the complainant, then it is

A   Determined by HMT

B   Always determined by the courts

C   Binding on the firm

D   Not binding on the firm

29. Which of the following is true?

A   The maximum payout of the Financial Ombudsman Service is £48,000 plus costs

B   The maximum payout of the Financial Services Compensation Scheme is £100,000

C   The maximum fine for market abuse is £1,000,000

D   The maximum payout of the Financial Ombudsman Service is £100,000 plus costs

30. For market abuse to have occurred

A   There must be intention

B   There must be intention and effect

C   There must be effect

D   There need not be effect

31. Which of the following statements about the Joint Money Laundering Steering Group is true?

A   It explains, via guidance notes, how to apply the statutory regulations relating to money laundering

B   It is a division of the FSA

C   It only applies to non-UK firms passporting into the UK

D   It relates to market abuse

32. Which of the following is false in respect of the Money Laundering Regulations?

A   Simplified due diligence procedures should be used for politically exposed persons

B   The Regulations apply to financial institutions and credit institutions

C   Where the client is introduced by an authorised firm, the firm can rely on the introducer for identification

D   Firms must take a risk-based approach to money laundering prevention

33. Which two of the following types of documentation would be appropriate for a firm to use to identify its trust clients for money laundering purposes?

      I   A passport or driving licence

      II   A certificate of incorporation and evidence of the company's registered address

      III   A copy of the latest report and accounts

      IV   A trust deed

A   III and IV

B   II and III

C   I and IV

D   I and III

34. Which one of the following is not one of the six desired outcomes specified by the FSA in its TCF (Treating Customers Fairly) initiative?

A   Products and services marketed and sold in the retail market are at lowest cost to the consumer

B   Consumers are provided with clear information and are kept appropriately informed before, during and after the point of sale.

C   Where consumers receive advice, the advice is suitable and takes account of their circumstances.

D   Consumers do not face unreasonable post-sale barriers imposed by firms to change product, switch provider, submit a claim or make a complaint.

Answers

1. **D** The transfer of responsibility for regulation of banking moved from the Bank of England to the FSA in 1998

    See Section 1.1.2 of your Study Text

2. **D** The Information Commissioner maintains a public registry of data controllers

    See Section 5 of your Study Text

3. **D** S150 is for breach of a rule. S71 is used when a firm has used an unapproved person

    See Section 6.1.2 of your Study Text

4. **A** Although a breach of DPA 1998 is a criminal offence, there is no option of a jail sentence

    See Section 5 of your Study Text

5. **C** Promoting the competence of investment advisers will hopefully follow on from the statutory objectives, but is not itself one of the four set statutory objectives

    See Section 2.2 of your Study Text

6. **A** FSMA 2000 was drafted by HM Treasury and is enforced by the FSA

    See Section 1.1 of your Study Text

7. **B** The correct wording is 'required functions'

    See Section 2.4 of your Study Text

8. **A** Placement involves getting the dirty cash into the system initially, layering involves many transactions in an attempt to disguise its true origins, and integration is the process during which the clean funds are re-entered into the system

    See Section 3.2 of your Study Text

9. **C** Market abuse is a civil offence and as such the person found guilty cannot be imprisoned

    See Section 4.3 of your Study Text

10. **B** Money laundering regulation is an important topic

    I   True – It is a requirement that institutions have procedures for checking the identity of clients

    II   True – The institution may need to enquire as to the source of funds

    III   True – Reporting suspicions is an important part of the legislation

    IV   False – You are not expected to assist the police in the arrest of the suspect

    See Section 3.8 of your Study Text

11. **D** Compensation is paid by the FSCS where the company concerned is or is likely to become insolvent

    See Section 6.3 of your Study Text

12.	**A**	The SEC is the regulator in the US. Whilst RIEs are exempt, membership alone is not a 'means of obtaining authorisation'. ICMA regulates the Eurobond market

See Section 2.3 of your Study Text

13.	**C**	The Treasury is responsible for the legislation

See Section 2.1 of your Study Text

14.	**C**	The legislation is the responsibility of the Treasury, but the investigation and prosecution of the offence is the responsibility of the Department for Business, Innovation and Skills

See Section 4.2 of your Study Text

15.	**B**	Layering is one of the stages of the typical money laundering process

Placement: getting the money into the financial system

Layering: separating the money from its illegal origin

Integration: process is complete, the money has been laundered and looks as if it has come from a legitimate source

See Section 3.2 of your Study Text

16.	**D**	The FSMA 2000 introduced statutory regulation – moving away from the earlier 'self-regulation within a statutory framework'

See Section 1.1 of your Study Text

17.	**D**	The Serious Organised Crime Agency (SOCA), previously known as the National Criminal Intelligence Service (NCIS), is the government body that co-ordinates money laundering enquiries

See Section 3.5.1 of your Study Text

18.	**D**	Financial Services Authority can remove approval from an approved person

See Section 2.4 of your Study Text

19.	**C**	The maximum amount the FSCS pays in relation to protected investments is 100% of the first £50,000.

See Section 6.3 of your Study Text

20.	**A**	The Financial Services Compensation Scheme pays out when the firm becomes insolvent or is likely to become insolvent

See Section 6.3 of your Study Text

21.	**D**	The maximum FSCS compensation for protected investments is £50,000.

See Section 6.3 of your Study Text

22.	**D**	The offence of market abuse covers UK markets and the main EEA exchanges

See Section 4.3 of your Study Text

23.　C　There needs to be a written procedure on how to handle complaints, and the client must be informed on the next stage of the complaints procedure if they are not satisfied. Complaints need to be handled by a sufficiently senior person

See Section 6.1 of your Study Text

24.　D　All of the options are correct. Be aware of the legislation regarding insider dealing and the defences that can be used

See Section 4.2 of your Study Text

25.　B　The Complaints Commissioner investigates individual complaints against the FSA itself

See Section 6.2 of your Study Text

26.　A　Set up by, but independent from, the FSA

See Section 6.2 of your Study Text

27.　D　The service is not available to all clients. It is only available to eligible complainants, i.e. private individuals or organisations with a turnover of less than £1m. Professional clients who have opted down to become retail clients are not eligibile

See Section 6.2 of your Study Text

28.　D　If the complaining customers refuses to accept the outcome of the FOS investigation, then it is not binding on the firm. Instead, the complainant may choose to take or not to take their case to courts

See Section 6.2 of your Study Text

29.　D　The maximum payout by the Ombudsman is £100,000 plus costs

See Section 6.2 of your Study Text

30.　C　It is possible to have abused a market without intention to do so through, for example, negligence. The legislation is effect-based

See Section 4.3 of your Study Text

31.　A　The guidance notes are just that: they are there for guidance. The JMLSG is not part of the FSA

See Section 3.3 of your Study Text

32.　A　It is permissible for one authorised firm to rely on the written assurance of another authorised firm for money laundering identification purposes. The position of PEPs can make them vulnerable to corruption, and enhanced due diligence is therefore appropriate

See Section 3.8 of your Study Text

33.　A　A passport or driving licence would help identify an individual and a certificate of incorporation would identify a corporate client only and not a trust client

See Section 3.8 of your Study Text

34.   **A**   To sell products at 'lowest cost' is not one of the six consumer outcomes specified by the FSA. The second outcome starts with similar words, and is as follows: 'Products and services marketed and sold in the retail market are designed to meet the needs of identified consumer groups and are targeted accordingly'.

See Section 2.6 of your Study Text

8. Taxation and Trusts

Questions

1. Which one of the following is not a chargeable disposal for capital gains tax purposes?

   A Sale of gilts

   B Sale of property

   C Gift of shares to one's brother

   D Sale of shares to a company pursuant to a share repurchase scheme approved by the shareholders in general meeting

2. From and to which dates does the fiscal year run?

   A 1 April to 31 March

   B 5 April to 6 April

   C 6 April to 5 April

   D 5 April to 5 April

3. CGT is not levied on

   A Sale of shares

   B Sale of gilts

   C Sale of second home

   D Sale of futures

4. Which of the following transfers is exempt from inheritance tax?

   A Gift to spouse or civil partner

   B Gift to children

   C Gift made one month before death

   D Gifts between siblings

5. Why would it be advantageous to give away your assets prior to your death?

   A To avoid capital gains tax

   B To avoid inheritance tax

   C To avoid stamp duty

   D To avoid income tax

6. ✓ **Which of the following are not exempt from CGT?**

    A   Gilts

    B   An individual's main residence

    Ⓒ   Antiques

    D   Wasting assets

7. ✗ **Bond interest paid to holders has tax deducted at source of**

    Ⓐ   10%

    B   20%

    C   32½%

    D   40%

8. ✗ **What is an individual's annual exemption for capital gains tax for the fiscal year 2010/2011?**

    A   £6,035

    Ⓑ   £6,475

    C   £10,100

    D   £325,000

9. ✗ **Which of the following allowances/exemptions can be carried forward one year?**

    A   Personal allowance under income tax

    B   Annual exemption under CGT

    C   Annual exemption under inheritance tax

    Ⓓ   Small gifts exemption under inheritance tax

10. ✓ **A widower makes a gift of £100,000 to each of his two children. This is a 'potentially exempt transfer'. How long must he live for there to be no tax payable in respect of these transfers?**

    A   Three years

    B   Five years

    Ⓒ   Seven years

    D   Nine years

11. ✓ **What is the maximum gift without Inheritance Tax implications that a parent can make in consideration of the marriage of a daughter?**

    A   £1,000

    B   £2,500

    Ⓒ   £5,000

    D   £10,000

12. ✕ **What additional liability to income tax exists for an individual in respect of UK dividends where the cash amount of dividend received was £600 and total other earnings are £19,600?**

    A Nil

    Ⓑ £60

    C £67

    D £150

13. ✓ **What causes a capital gains tax payment?**

    A Chargeable purchase

    B End of the tax year

    C Issue by the Government of each month's RPI figures

    Ⓓ Chargeable disposal of a chargeable asset by a chargeable person

14. ✕ **The carry-forward period for losses on equity shares for capital gains tax purposes is**

    A Six months

    Ⓑ Two years

    C Indefinite

    D Six years

15. ✓ **On which of the following are losses on disposal not allowable for capital gains tax purposes?**

    Ⓐ Gilts

    B Traded options

    C Financial futures

    D A holiday home in Florida

16. ✕ **Farid transfers a holding of shares to his wife. Which of the following is true?**

    A Capital gains tax is payable by Farid on this transfer

    B Capital gains tax is payable by Farid's wife on this transfer

    Ⓒ No tax is payable currently, since this is a potentially exempt transfer between husband and wife

    D No tax is payable currently, but Farid's wife is deemed to have acquired the shares at the original cost to Farid

17. ✕ **From the following list, which will be taxed as earned income?**

    A Taxable benefits in kind

    B Building Society interest

    Ⓒ Dividend income

    D Income from land or property

18. A man transferred £500,000 to his wife (UK domiciled) and then died three years later. When is inheritance tax payable on the amount transferred?

   Ⓐ Immediately

   B When the wife dies

   C No tax is payable

   D After four more years from date of death

19. In 2010/11, Jamal earns £24,000 per annum. In the same year, she receives £1,000 gross income from a building society and £1,000 in dividends. How much extra income tax does she have to pay on the dividends?

   A £nil

   Ⓑ £111

   C £361

   D £525

20. If Devraj makes a gift of £7,000 to his ex-wife Hamsa, how long does he have to have given it before his death so that it is not taxable?

   A The gift is exempt

   B One year

   C Five years

   Ⓓ Seven years

21. If Mr and Mrs Lefevre have not used up their inheritance tax exemption for last year, what is the most they can give as a gift in 2010/11 between them, utilising only the IHT annual exemption?

   A £3,000

   Ⓑ £6,000

   C £9,000

   D £12,000

22. Paul has made a loss on selling shares of £5,000. For how long can he carry this loss forward for offset in the future?

   Ⓐ Two years

   B Six years

   C Seven years

   D Indefinitely

23. How many gifts of £250 can be made without an inheritance tax liability?

A 12

B 24

C 32

D No limit

24. The VAT rate is 0% on all of the following, except

A Newspapers

B Children's clothes

C Electrical goods

D Food bought in a supermarket

25. The financial year 2010/11 runs from

A 6 April 2010 to 5 April 2011

B 1 January 2010 to 31 December 2010

C 1 April 2010 to 31 March 2011

D Any 12 month period decided by the company

26. Which of the following is not a participant in a trust?

A Depositary

B Settlor

C Beneficiary

D Trustee

Answers

1. **A**   Gilts are always exempt from capital gains tax. Answer D may sound very complicated, but it is just a sale of shares and therefore may be liable to CGT

    See Section 2.2 of your Study Text

2. **C**   The fiscal year relates to a year for which a personal tax calculation is performed

    See Section 1.2 of your Study Text

3. **B**   Gilts, main home and wasting assets are exempt CGT

    See Section 2.2 of your Study Text

4. **A**   Gifts between spouses or civil partners are always exempt from IHT

    See Section 3.3 of your Study Text

5. **B**   Unless assets are gifted seven years or more prior to death, they could be chargeable to IHT

    See Section 3.2 of your Study Text

6. **C**   Sale of antiques represents a chargeable disposal for purposes of CGT

    See Section 2.2 of your Study Text

7. **B**   Interest income from bonds and bank accounts suffers 20% tax at source, except for gilts, which are normally received gross

    See Section 1.3 of your Study Text

8. **C**   The annual exemption for capital gains tax is in addition to the personal allowance for income tax

    See Section 2.3 of your Study Text

9. **C**   The annual exemption is available for carry forward for one year only

    See Section 3.5 of your Study Text

10. **C**   There is no tax due on a potentially exempt transfer, once the donor has survived for seven years following the gift

    See Section 3.2 of your Study Text

11. **C**   Each parent may make a gift of £5,000, which will be exempt on consideration of marriage

    See Section 3.4 of your Study Text

12. **A**   The individual is a basic rate taxpayer. There is no further liability on dividends for a basic rate taxpayer, as a 10% notional tax credit has been received on the dividend

    See Section 1.4 of your Study Text

13. **D**   Capital gains tax is paid on a chargeable disposal if there is not enough unused losses or annual exemption to set off against the gain

    See Section 2.1 of your Study Text

14. **C** Carry forward of CGT losses is indefinite. Indexation cannot be used to create or increase a loss

See Section 2.3 of your Study Text

15. **A** Gains on gilts are exempt from CGT and accordingly losses are not allowable

See Section 2.2 of your Study Text

16. **D** Transfers between husband and wife are deemed to be no loss/gain transactions

See Section 2.2 of your Study Text

17. **A** Taxable benefits in kind are taxed as earned income

Note: income from property is unearned income

See Section 1 of your Study Text

18. **C** No tax is payable on the man's death nor, if at her death, the wife's total assets are lower than the combination of her own nil-rate band and that of her husband's. However, if at her death she has assets in excess of the combined nil-rate bands then IHT will be due on that excess. This also assumes that the wife is UK domiciled, but take this to be the case unless the question states otherwise

See Section 3.3 of your Study Text

19. **A** The dividends are received with a 10% tax credit which means that Jamal's liability to basic rate tax is removed: she will have no further tax to pay as long as her total income remains below the higher rate band

See Section 1.4 of your Study Text

20. **D** As Hamsa is the ex-wife of Devraj, this gift will not benefit from the spouse's transfer exemption. It will be a potentially exempt transfer and requires seven full years to expire before the gift becomes exempt

See Section 3.2 of your Study Text

21. **D** The couple will be able to give £6,000 each. £6,000 × 2 = £12,000 and this will use up the annual exemptions. There is no limit on the amount that the couple can give away, but this will be potentially subject to tax

See Section 3.5 of your Study Text

22. **D** Losses for CGT can be carried forward indefinitely

See Section 2.3 of your Study Text

23. **D** There is no limit on the number of £250 gifts that may be made

See Section 3.4 of your Study Text

24. **C** All the others are exempt from VAT

See Section 6 of your Study Text

25. **C** Be careful not to confuse the financial year with the fiscal year (i.e. answer A)

See Section 7 of your Study Text

26.   **A**   'Depositary' is the name used to describe the trustee of an OEIC

            See Section 8.2 of your Study Text

axation and Trusts – Answers

Practice
Examinations

Contents

Practice Examinations	Page Number	
	Questions	Answers
Practice Examination 1	85	95
Practice Examination 2	99	109
Practice Examination 3	115	125
Practice Examination 4	129	139
Practice Examination 5	143	153

Practice Examination 1

50 Questions in 1 Hour

1. × **Which of the following are primarily the clients of the retail sector?**

   A Personal and institutional investors

   B Institutional investors

   C Commercial businesses

   D Personal investors

2. ✓ **Which of the following has responsibility for looking after investments on behalf of fund managers, pension funds and insurance companies?**

   A Trustee

   B Registrar

   C Depository

   D Custodian

3. ✓ **Which of the following sets interest rates in the UK?**

   A Financial Services Authority

   B Governor of the Bank of England

   C HM Treasury

   D Monetary Policy Committee

4. ✓ **Creation of credit occurs due to**

   A Issuance of notes and coins into the economy

   B Bank lending

   C Increase in inflation

   D Increasing exports

5. × **Which of the following is most likely to benefit from inflation?**

   A Savers

   B Borrowers

   C Exporters

   D Retired pensioners

6. What will be the effect of completing an IR85 on the interest paid to an investor?

A Interest will be credited monthly

(B) The amount of interest credited will reduce

C Interest will be credited annually

D Interest will be paid gross with no deduction of tax

7. An investor who pays tax at 40% invests £20,000 in a bank. £3,000 of this is placed in a Cash ISA and the remaining sum into a high interest account. Both pay 4.5% gross. What will be the monetary sum received at the end of the year?

(A) £540

B £594

C £747

D £900

8. How often are Treasury Bill tenders held?

A Daily

B Weekly

C Monthly

D Annually

9. What is the interest on a bond known as?

A Yield

B Dividend

C Coupon

D Debenture

10. A small investor with a diversified portfolio is least likely to directly invest in which of the following types of property investment?

A Property Bond

B Property Unit Trust

C Property Company Shares

D Commercial Property

11. With which of the following is the term 'forward' most commonly associated?

A Equities

B Unit trusts

C Foreign exchange

D Insurance

12. Which of the following is the main exchange for traded options?

A NYSE Liffe

B London Stock Exchange

C LCH.Clearnet

D Euroclear

13. The FTSE 100 index is comprised of

A Top 100 performing companies on the LSE

B All LSE equities

C 100 Companies selected by the Financial Times

D Approximately the top 100 companies on LSE based on market capitalisation

14. Which of the following is true of the Dow Jones Index?

A Provides a narrow view of the US equity market

B Provides a broad view of the US equity market

C Provides a narrow view of the US commodities market

D Provides a broad view of the US commodities market

15. What is the function of underwriters?

A To issue new shares of a company

B To buy shares not subscribed for

C To cancel issued shares

D To assist companies in finding buyers for their shares

16. What is the difference between a secured and unsecured loan?

A A life contract that will pay off the debt in case of default

B A secured loan has a contractual agreement to ensure payment of the debt linked to the borrower's assets. An unsecured loan does not

C A third party agrees to be jointly liable to the debt

D There is no difference in risk to the lender

17. If a company is proposing to change its constitution, what minimum percentage of eligible shareholders must vote in favour?

A 51%

B 60%

C 75%

D 90%

18. What is the minimum number of years that a company must have been trading to gain a full listing on LSE?

   A   One year

   B   Two years

   Ⓒ   Three years

   D   Five years

19. Which of the following is a disadvantage of listing?

   Ⓐ   May be subject to a takeover bid

   B   Must pay a dividend to shareholders

   C   Founding shareholders must sell their entire holding

   D   Directors must be given free shares

20. Which of the following is the most likely reason for gaining a listing on the Alternative Investment Market?

   A   Lower costs than borrowing

   B   Gain overseas contracts

   C   Takeover another company

   Ⓓ   Access to capital

21. When a company issues cumulative preference shares, which of the following is the true consequence?

   Ⓐ   Dividends roll up to be paid on redemption

   B   If a dividend cannot be paid due to lack of profits, then the dividend will still be payable at a future date when the company has sufficient funds

   C   The dividend accumulates until the investor elects to take payment

   D   The dividend rises each year and takes part in exceptional profits of the company

22. Which of the following is an example of a mandatory corporate action where the investor will receive fully paid up shares?

   A   Bonus issue

   B   Dividend

   Ⓒ   Rights issue

   D   Open offer

23. A life policy which has a sum assured of £120,000 throughout the term of the policy is known as

   A   Non-profit

   Ⓑ   Traditional with-profit

   C   Unitised with-profit

   D   Unit-linked

24. A gilt with five or less years left to run is known as

   A Short
   B Medium
   C Long
   D Repo

25. A 4% £100 nominal bond has a market price of £70. What is the current flat yield?

   A 4%
   B 4.5%
   C 5.71%
   D 7%

26. Which of the following is an advantage of a corporate bond?

   A Mid-term payment
   B Ability to alter coupon frequency
   C Normally fixed term to redemption
   D Rebate for non-taxpayers on initial capital

27. Which of the following is the best term to describe an exchange of a fixed interest payment for a floating interest payment?

   A Forward rate agreement
   B Interest rate future
   C Swap
   D Repo

28. You are the writer of call options in XYZ plc. What is the nature of your commitment?

   A You are the buyer of the right to sell shares at a fixed price
   B You have bought the right to sell XYZ plc shares at a fixed price on an agreed date and you have received a premium
   C You are the buyer of the right to buy shares at a fixed price
   D You have sold the right to buy XYZ plc shares at a fixed price on an agreed date and you have received a premium

29. Which of the following is a closed-ended fund?

   A An investment trust because it has a fixed number of shares
   B A unit trust because it has a fixed capital structure
   C An investment company with variable capital because it has a limited number of investors
   D An ISA unit trust because it has fixed tax benefits

30. Which of the following is true of a unit trust?

    A The Trustee is the legal owner of the trust's assets

    B The Trustee is responsible for legal and beneficial ownership of the trust's assets

    C An authorised depository is the legal owner of the assets on behalf of the Trustee

    D The unit holder is the legal owner of the trust's assets

31. An investment trust is bought in the same way as

    A Unit trust

    B OEIC

    C Equities

    D Insurance bonds

32. Which of the following is responsible for the independent supervision of the board of an OEIC?

    A FSA

    B Depositary

    C Trustee

    D Treasury

33. Which of the following is traded on the Stock Exchange?

    A Unit trust

    B OEIC

    C Insurance bonds

    D ETFs

34. Which of the following is responsible for keeping the register of shareholders for an OEIC?

    A ACD

    B Depository

    C Trustee

    D Registrar

35. What percentage of a Real Estate Investment Trust's profits must be distributed to shareholders in order to avoid Corporation Tax?

    A 60%

    B 70%

    C 80%

    D 90%

36. Which of the following is an objective given to the Financial Services Authority under the Financial Services and Markets Act 2000?

A Maintain confidence in the UK financial system

B Reduce the need for fraud investigations

C To ensure an adequate degree of protection for those working in the finance industry

D Promote public awareness of the Stock Exchange

37. If a firm's Anti-Money Laundering Officer has grounds to believe that a report should be passed on to the authorities, which of the following would they refer to?

A FSA

B Joint Money Laundering Steering Group

C Serious Organised Crime Agency

D Treasury

38. Which of the following would constitute insider dealing?

A Dealing on information believed, with reasonable grounds, to be widely available to the public

B Dealing to repay a debt regardless of the information held

C Dealing but not making a profit

D Dealing on unpublished information that is unavailable to the public

39. Under the Data Protection Principles of the Data Protection Act 1998, how long may information be retained?

A 12 months

B 3 years

C 5 years

D As long as necessary for its purpose

40. If a firm investigates a material complaint, what must it do when providing a final response to the complainant?

A It must refer the detail of the complaint to the FSA within 48 hours

B It must offer the complainant an ex-gratia payment of no less than £200

C It must advise the complainant that they can refer the matter to the Financial Ombudsman Service if they are not happy with the firm's final response

D They must take independent legal advice before accepting the final response

41. An investor loses £35,000 which he placed in investments with a firm that has not been subject to FSA authorisation and has now been wound up as insolvent. How much can the investor claim from the Financial Services Compensation Scheme?

A Nothing

B £31,500

C £34,500

D £35,000

42. Which of the following is exempt from further liability to Capital Gains Tax?

A Equities

B Unit Trust

C Options

D Equity ISA

43. What is the earliest age that an investor may open a Cash ISA?

A 15

B 16

C 17

D 18

44. At what age will the child be able to make withdrawals from a Child Trust Fund?

A 15

B 16

C 17

D 18

45. Which of the following is also known a Defined Benefit Scheme?

A Money purchase

B Final salary

C Protected rights

D Retirement annuity

46. Which of the following is not subject to Capital Gains Tax?

A Eurobond

B Unit Trust

C OEIC

D Gilt

47. Which of the following is always exempt from inheritance tax?

   A   Children

   B   Spouse

   C   Parents

   D   Siblings

48. Who is the legal owner of a trust's assets?

   A   Settlor

   B   Trustee

   C   Creator

   D   Beneficiary

49. A lender X quotes an interest rate on a loan of 12%. Interest will be charged monthly. What is the annual equivalent rate?

   A   12.0%

   B   12.68%

   C   12.84%

   D   11.4%

50. What is the main reason why the UK mortgage market is bigger than in most other EU countries?

   A   More people in the UK tend to own their own home

   B   Renting is not as popular in the EU as in the UK

   C   Mortgages are controlled in some EU states

   D   In some EU countries, each mortgage must be individually approved by Government

Answers

1. **D** Personal investors are the primary clients in the retail sector

    See Chapter 1 Section 8.1 of your Study Text

2. **D** A custodian is responsible for looking after the assets of fund managers and so on

    See Chapter 1 Section 3.9 of your Study Text

3. **D** The Monetary Policy Committee sets short-term interest rates in the UK

    See Chapter 1 Section 2.1 of your Study Text

4. **B** Bank lending leads to credit creation

    See Chapter 1 Section 1.7 of your Study Text

5. **B** Borrowers are likely to benefit most from inflation

    See Chapter 1 Section 1.8.3 of your Study Text

6. **D** Interest is paid gross without deduction of tax

    See Chapter 8 Section 1.4 of your Study Text

7. **C** £3,000 x 4.5% = £135 and £17,000 x 4.5% = £765

    £765 x 80% = £612 (This is the amount received minus tax deducted at source)

    So the monetary amount received at the end of the year will be £135 + £612

    There will be a further tax liability of £153 to pay at a later point as the investor is a 40% taxpayer

    See Chapter 4 Section 1 and Chapter 6 Section 1.1 of your Study Text

8. **B** Treasury Bill auctions are held weekly (Note: the question wrongly asked 'How often are Treasury Bill tenders held by the Bank of England?' It is the DMO who hold the tender)

    See Chapter 2 Section 12.2 of your Study Text

9. **C** Coupon is the name for interest on a bond

    See Chapter 2 Section 10.2.4 of your Study Text

10. **D** Commercial property is the least likely investment

    See Chapter 4 Section 2.1 of your Study Text

11. **C** Forward rates are commonly associated with the currency market

    See Chapter 1 Section 7.3 of your Study Text

12. **A** NYSE Liffe is the main exchange for traded options

    See Chapter 1 Section 6.2 of your Study Text

13. **D**   Market capitalisation determines entry to and exit from the FTSE 100

        See Chapter 2 Section 6.2 of your Study Text

14. **A**   The DJIA represents 30 US industrial shares, selected by committee, and therefore provides only a narrow view on the US equity market

        See Chapter 2 Section 6.2 of your Study Text

15. **B**   Underwriters provide a guarantee for the issuing companies against unsold shares

        See Chapter 2, Section 3.4.3 of your Study Text

16. **B**   There is a contract linking payment of the debt to the borrower's assets

        See Chapter 4 Section 5.3 of your Study Text

17. **C**   A Special Resolution is required. 75% of those voting must vote in favour

        See Chapter 2 Section 1.3 of your Study Text

18. **C**   A three year track record is required to gain full listing

        See Chapter 2 Section 4.3 of your Study Text

19. **A**   Listed companies may be subject to a takeover bid

        See Chapter 2 Section 4.2 of your Study Text

20. **D**   The major benefit of becoming AIM quoted is access to new capital

        See Chapter 2 Section 5 of your Study Text

21. **B**   'Cumulative' means that, if the dividend is unpaid, it will accumulate to be paid in a subsequent year

        See Chapter 2 Section 1.6 of your Study Text

22. **A**   Bonus issues are mandatory and lead to fully paid up shares being issued

        See Chapter 2 Section 3.2 of your Study Text

23. **A**   A sum assured which remains unchanged is characteristic of a non-profit policy

        See Chapter 4 Section 7 of your Study Text

24. **A**   A gilt which has five or less year to run is known as a short

        See Chapter 2 Section 10.4 of your Study Text

25. **C** $4/70 \times 100 = 5.71\%$. Flat yield is coupon/price x 100

        See Chapter 2 Section 11.7 of your Study Text

26. **C**   Corporate bonds normally have a fixed term to redemption

        See Chapter 2 Section 11.1 of your Study Text

27. C A swap is an exchange of different types of interest payment for an agreed amount at an agreed price

   See Chapter 3 Section 5 of your Study Text

28. D You are the writer, so you sold the option to someone else. As it is a call option, it gives them the right to buy shares from you at an agreed price. You were paid a premium to undertake this obligation

   See Chapter 3 Section 3.3.2 of your Study Text

29. A An Investment trust is a closed ended fund. Companies generally, except OEICs, are closed-ended

   See Chapter 5 Section 4.1 of your Study Text

30. A The trustee of a unit trust is the legal owner of the trust's assets. The beneficial owners are the unitholders

   See Chapter 5 Section 2.1 of your Study Text

31. C An investment trust is bought in the same way as other equities, i.e. through a stock broker

   See Chapter 5 Section 4.2 of your Study Text

32. B The Depository supervises the ACD. The FSA is the regulator of OEICs

   See Chapter 5 Section 3.2 of your Study Text

33. D ETFs are exchange traded funds and so, as their name implies, trade on the Stock Exchange

   See Chapter 5 Section 5 of your Study Text

34. A ACD is the registrar for an OEIC

   See Chapter 5 Section 3.3 of your Study Text

35. D 90% of profits need to be paid to investors, to benefit from the Corporation Tax exemption

   See Chapter 5 Section 7 of your Study Text

36. A Maintain confidence in the UK financial system

   See Chapter 7 Section 2.2 of your Study Text

37. C Referrals would be made to the Serious Organised Crime Agency

   See Chapter 7 Section 3.5.1 of your Study Text

38. D Dealing on information that is not available to the public. The others are defences against insider dealing

   See Chapter 7 Section 4.2 of your Study Text

39. D Information may only be retained for as long as is necessary for its purpose

   See Chapter 7 Section 5 of your Study Text

40. C Reference to the FOS must be made in the final response to the complainant

   See Chapter 7 Section 6.1.1 of your Study Text

41. **A**   Given that the firm was not authorised by the FSA, there is no compensation payment

See Chapter 7 Section 6.3 of your Study Text

42. **D**   Equity ISAs would have no CGT liability

See Chapter 8 Section 2.2 of your Study Text

43. **B**   16 years is the earliest age that it is possible to open a cash ISA

See Chapter 6 Section 1.1 of your Study Text

44. **D**   Withdrawals are not permitted until after the child's 18th birthday

See Chapter 6 Section 2 of your Study Text

45. **B**   Final salary schemes are also known as Defined Benefit Schemes

See Chapter 4 Section 3.3.1 of your Study Text

46. **D**   Gilts are exempt from CGT

See Chapter 8 Section 2.2 of your Study Text

47. **B**   Spouses are exempt from IHT

See Chapter 8 Section 3.3 of your Study Text

48. **B**   The trustee is the legal owner of the assets from a trust

See Chapter 8 Section 8.2 of your Study Text

49. **B**   1% monthly. $1.01^{12} = 1.1268$, so 12.68%

See Chapter 4 Section 5.2 of your Study Text

50. **A**   UK residents typically prefer to buy rather than rent

See Chapter 4 Section 6 of your Study Text

Practice Examination 2

50 Questions in 1 Hour

1. Which of the following is associated with the financial term 'forward'?

   A   Insurance transaction

   B   Foreign exchange transaction

   C   Equity transaction

   D   Unit trust transaction

2. Which of the following is true of preference shares?

   A   They always receive a dividend even if there are no profits

   B   The dividend is never cumulative

   C   A dividend level is fixed as a percentage of their nominal value on issue

   D   Holders receive interest but the dividend is retained for the benefit of the company

3. Which of the following is likely to benefit most from high inflation?

   A   Saver

   B   Earner of a fixed income

   C   Borrower

   D   Exporters

4. Which of the following describes the creation of credit?

   A   Bank lending more than it has in its reserves

   B   Businesses paying creditors promptly

   C   Paying by cash rather than cheque

   D   Treasury printing more notes and coins

5. Which of the following is the purpose of the Monetary Policy Committee?

   A   To control inflation through the use of interest rates

   B   Recommend an inflation target to the Treasury

   C   Set the current rate of inflation

   D   To measure the current level of money supply

6. Which of the following is a function of the Bank of England?

    A Act as the Government's banker

    B Regulate building societies

    C Recommend an inflation target to the Treasury

    D Approve the authorisation of financial services firms

7. Why was the 'extraMARK' platform developed by the London Stock Exchange?

    A To trade individual stock options

    B To trade commodities

    C To trade Exchange Traded Funds (ETFs)

    D To trade futures

8. On which exchange do the 'soft commodities' trade?

    A NYSE Liffe

    B London Stock Exchange

    C London Metal Exchange

    D ICE Futures

9. Which of the following is true for a private limited company?

    A If it wishes to issue shares to the public, the issue must have approval from Companies House

    B 75% of shareholders must vote in favour of issuing shares to the public

    C It is not possible to issue shares to the public

    D It is possible to issue shares to the public but a maximum block of only 1,000 shares per person can be issued

10. A firm's anti-money laundering regulations typically require a new individual client to provide identity showing the person's name, and what else?

    A Age

    B Address

    C Date of birth

    D Place of birth

11. Which of the following carry full voting entitlement?

    A Preference shares

    B Debentures

    C A Class shares

    D Ordinary shares

12. Which of the following is true following a capitalisation issue?

   A The number of shares held will change

   B The price per shares will remain the same

   C There will be a repayment to the shareholder of capital

   D The shareholder will have to sell some of his/her holding

13. How would a certificated holding be settled?

   A Through Book Entry Transfer

   B Through providing a share certificate and signed transfer form

   C By notifying the registrar

   D By filling in the form of renunciation on the back of the certificate

14. Which of the following is an advantage of a company gaining a listing?

   A It will be more accountable to its shareholders

   B It must meet the LSE information requirements

   C It has greater access to capital

   D It has more control over how it spends it capital

15. A bond has a coupon of 7% maturing in 2015. Its current price is 112. What is the bond's flat yield at this point in time?

   A 7.0%

   B 6.25%

   C 7.95%

   D 12.0%

16. A firm receives a complaint. What is the maximum time the firm has to send a holding or final response?

   A Five days

   B Ten days

   C Four weeks

   D Eight weeks

17. Which of the following is the best definition of a gilt?

   A Short-term debt issued at a discount to par

   B Debt instrument issued by a company with a fixed coupon

   C Debt instrument issued by the Government to fund spending in excess of receipts

   D Debt instrument issued by local government to fund spending in excess of statutory funding

18. A bond which is issued outside of the jurisdiction of a single government is most appropriately referred to as a

    A Eurobond

    B Japanese Government Bond

    C Bund

    D OATs

19. How are gilts issued?

    A By auction through the DMO

    B By auction conducted on LSE

    C By fixed offer through the LSE

    D By placing through the LSE

20. A short gilt is a gilt with a life of less than

    A One year

    B Three years

    C Five years

    D Seven years

21. An agreement to deliver a standard quantity of a specified asset at a future date at a price agreed today is a

    A Put

    B Call

    C Forward

    D Future

22. An Open Ended Investment Company is a collective investment fund

    A Whose shares are single-priced

    D That trades at a discount to its net asset value

    B That has a fixed lifespan

    C That has a fixed amount of share capital

23. For a retail bank account, it is possible to determine the net rate from the gross equivalent amount by

    A Deducting 10% savings tax from the gross amount

    B Deducting 20% income tax from the gross amount

    C An R85 adjustment

    D A P11D adjustment

24. What would the interest rate typically be on a secured loan compared to an unsecured loan for a similar amount?

   A   Higher
   B   Lower
   C   The same
   D   Not possible to determine

25. Which of the following is the most accurate description of a mortgage?

   A   A loan to purchase property
   B   An equitable charge to the borrower
   C   Assigning the repayment vehicle to the lender
   D   Providing security for a loan

26. A capped mortgage where the borrower pays no more than a maximum amount can be described as

   A   Discounted rate
   B   Variable rate
   C   Five-year fixed rate
   D   Base rate tracker

27. Which is a characteristic of a non-profit whole of life policy?

   A   A fixed sum assured
   B   Exempt from inheritance tax on payment
   C   A return linked to stock market performance
   D   Would accept an additional life assured

28. Under a stakeholder pension plan opened in the current year, what is the maximum charge that can be made for transfers into or out of the fund?

   A   1% of fund value at time of transfer
   B   No charges are allowed
   C   £20 net
   D   £20 gross

29. Which describes a pension scheme that will provide an income linked to earnings at or close to the retirement age?

   A   Contracted out money purchase scheme
   B   Executive pension plan
   C   Final salary scheme
   D   Deferred income scheme

30. What are the maximum annual charges that can be imposed on a stakeholder pension plan opened in the current year?

   A £100
   B 1.5% of the fund value
   C £1 per month
   D 1% of the bid/offer price

31. What is the minimum amount of net taxable profits that a REIT must distribute if it is to remain exempt from corporation tax?

   A 70%
   B 80%
   C 90%
   D 100%

32. Which of the following best describes the function of the Depositary in an OEIC?

   A Is responsible for the management of the OEIC and retaining the register
   B Is the point of contact for the sale and redemption of Shares
   C Has custody of the assets and oversees the ACD to ensure that it complies with the Instrument of Incorporation and prospectus
   D Is responsible for establishing a board of directors to run the OEIC

33. Which of the following are true of the process of incorporating a company in the UK?

   I   Any one person can form a company
   II   Certain forms must be completed and deposited with the Department for Business, Innovation & Skills
   III The Department for Business, Innovation & Skills is responsible for the Registrar of Companies
   IV   Companies are bound by the provisions of the various Companies Acts in force

   A I, II and III
   B I and IV
   C II, III and IV
   D III and IV

34. Whom should individual investors contact if they are interested in investing in investment trust shares?

   A Stock broker
   B London Stock Exchange
   C FSA
   D UKLA

35. The term 'closed-ended' applied to an investment trust indicates that it

A   Is not available to new retail investors

B   Has a fixed lifespan

C   Has a limited number of shares in issue

D   Cannot be advertised

36. What is the maximum amount that can be invested by a 25-year old investor in a cash ISA in 2010/11?

A   £3,000

B   £3,600

C   £5,100

D   £7,200

37. What does 'UCITS' stand for?

A   Unified Consolidated Investment Trading Service

B   Under-performing Corporate Institutions Tax System

C   Undertakings for Collective Investments in Transferable Securities

D   Unlimited Companies for Investments in Traded Swaps

38. Which of the following is not one of the FSA's statutory objectives?

A   Maintain confidence in the UK financial system

B   Promote public awareness of the financial system

C   Ensure the appropriate degree of protection for consumers

D   Prevent money laundering

39. Who would report a suspicious transaction to the Serious Organised Crime Agency?

A   The employee

B   The Money Laundering Reporting Officer (MLRO) of the firm

C   The firm's executive committee

D   The Joint Money Laundering Steering Group (JMLSG), after consulting with the firm's Compliance Department

40. What is the interest received on a bond called?

A   Yield

B   Coupon

C   Dividend

D   Debenture

41. A firm which has completed dealing with a material complaint must, as part of the final response,

    A   Offer an ex-gratia payment of at least £20 as a gesture of goodwill

    B   Send a copy of the complaints procedure

    C   Inform the complainant of their right to refer to FOS

    D   Inform with FSA within three working days of the detail of the complaint

42. How much money can a family invest each year into a Child Trust Fund (CTF) which will be tax free in respect of any earnings?

    A   £250

    B   £500

    C   £1,200

    D   £1,450

43. Which independent body regulates an OEIC?

    A   Financial Services Authority

    B   Depository

    C   Authorised Corporate Director

    D   Her Majesty's Treasury

44. With regard to life assurance, which of the following is true?

    A   Term assurance will normally have a surrender value

    B   Whole of life policies will only pay out if death occurs within a specified term

    C   With-profits policies guarantee a sum upon death plus a possible terminal bonus

    D   Unit-linked policies create a certain sum of money payable if death occurs within a specified term

45. Under which of the following circumstances would a claim be made on the Financial Services Compensation Scheme?

    A   Where the firm involved is declared insolvent

    B   Where an approved person working for the firm acted in a negligent manner

    C   Where an approved person working for the firm acted in a fraudulent manner

    D   Where the FSA have withdrawn the authorisation of the firm to conduct investment business

46. Which of the following is an index for the stock market of Germany?

    A   CAC

    B   DAX

    C   Mibtel

    D   Nikkei 225

47. You borrow some money from the bank and are quoted a rate of 8% payable quarterly. What is the Annual Equivalent Rate you will pay?

A   8.0%

B   7.76%

C   8.24%

D   2.0%

48. Which of the following best describes the function of a market maker?

A   To forecast the prices at which they will transact

B   Quote the size and price at which they will transact

C   They are not for profit organisations designed to create an orderly market

D   They will report trades via the SETS system

49. A lending banking is quoting a simple rate of interest on a loan, with no charges. The effective annual rate on the loan will be the same unless

A   Interest is paid in advance instead of in arrears

B   Interest is paid more often than once per year

C   The loan is secured

D   The loan is to a charity

50. What compensation would you expect if you lost £45,000 with an investment firm that had become insolvent?

A   £50,000

B   £43,500

C   £45,000

D   £40,500

Answers

1. **B** Forward transactions are commonly associated with the FX market where a deal is conducted at an agreed price and date in the future. This compares to a future which is an agreement to buy or sell a standard amount of a specified asset on a fixed date at a fixed price. Futures are tradable whereas forwards are not

   See Chapter 1 Section 7.3 of your Study Text

2. **C** The dividend on preference shares is a fixed dividend expressed as a percentage of nominal value. Preference shares are usually (but not always) cumulative. While the preference dividend must be paid before an ordinary dividend is paid and may be paid in years where the company has made no profits, preference shareholders have no automatic right to the dividend, which is paid at the discretion of the company

   See Chapter 2, Section 1.6 of your Study Text

3. **C** A saver will be earning a set amount of interest on his savings and high inflation will mean that his money can buy less and less as time goes by. This is even more the case for an earner or receiver of a fixed income such as a pensioner. In addition an exporter will sell his goods at a fixed price and this will also be eroded with high inflation. However a borrower is most likely to benefit since the amount owing will lose value in comparison to earnings (which tend to increase faster than inflation)

   See Chapter 1 Section 1.8.3 of your Study Text

4. **A** Banks lending more than reserves is the main method of credit creation. When a business pays its creditors promptly, it is simply paying what was is due into the system – which is not 'new' money. Paying in cash compared to a cheque is also not 'new' money. Although printing more notes and coins can contribute to creating credit, it is usually accompanied by the withdrawal of old notes and coins

   See Chapter 1 Section 1.7 of your Study Text

5. **A** The inflation target is set each year by The Chancellor to the Exchequer, not by the Bank. Nobody sets a rate of inflation – it is something which is measured. The Bank may well measure money supply but the question specifically relates to the Monetary Policy Committee whose function is indeed to control inflation through interest rates

   See Chapter 1 Section 2.1 of your Study Text

6. **A** It is the FSA that regulates building societies as well as the authorisation of financial firms. The Bank of England does not recommend an inflation target to the Treasury. (The Treasury has enough of its own economists who can do that!) The BoE, as a central bank, is indeed the Government's banker

   See Chapter 1 Section 2.1 of your Study Text

7. **C** The LSE developed the 'extraMARK' platform in order to allow Exchange Traded Funds to be traded on SETS

   See Chapter 5 Section 3.1 of your Study Text

8.　**A**　The London Stock Exchange is a market for securities. As its name suggests, the London Metal Exchange trades base metal derivatives, and ICE Futures is concerned with energy derivatives. Soft commodities are traded on NYSE Liffe

See Chapter 1 Section 5.1 of your Study Text

9.　**C**　It is not possible for a private limited company to issue shares to the public – full stop! Therefore all the other answers are 'red herrings'

See Chapter 2 Section 1.2 of your Study Text

10.　**B**　It is necessary to establish satisfactory evidence of identity. The name and address is typically a minimum requirement. How much identity information to ask for, and what to verify, are matters for the judgement of the firm, based on its assessment of risk

See Chapter 7 Section 3.8 of your Study Text

11.　**D**　Debentures are a form of debt set against fixed charges and as such have no voting rights. Normally, Preference shares have no voting rights but could acquire voting rights in circumstances where their dividend had not been paid for five years. Class A shares are shares in the company but specifically exclude voting rights. It is the ordinary shares of a company that carry full voting rights

See Chapter 2 Section 1.5 of your Study Text

12.　**A**　The number of shares will change as there will be more after the bonus issue but their price will fall proportionately to the increase in shares. Reserves are used to create the new shares but no money actually changes hands. There is no requirement for the shareholder to sell (nor buy) any of his holding

See Chapter 2 Section 3.2 of your Study Text

13.　**B**　The certificate and signed transfer form must be provided. The other answers are incorrect

See Chapter 2 Section 2.3.2 of your Study Text

14.　**C**　Neither being more accountable to shareholders nor being subject to information requirements from the LSE can be seen as an advantage. In addition, by listing itself, a company is likely to have less, and not more, control of how it spends its capital. However a listed company has greater access to capital than a non-listed company and hence this is an advantage

See Chapter 2 Section 4.1 of your Study Text

15.　**B**　Flat yield is calculated as (coupon divided by price) x 100. In this case it would be (7 / 112) x 100 = 6.25%

See Chapter 2, Section 11.7 of your Study Text

16.　**D**　A firm has to send a holding or final response within eight weeks

See Chapter 7 Section 6.1.1 of your Study Text

17.　**C**　Firstly, gilts can be short-term as well as long-term (for example, there has been the issue of a 50-year gilt in recent years). Secondly, gilts are issued by the government and not by companies nor by local authorities. They are debt instrument issued to finance the PSNCR

See Chapter 2 Section 10.1 of your Study Text

18. **A**   Japanese government bonds, Bunds and OATs are all issued by their respective governments (Japan, Germany and France) whereas a Eurobond is outside of a single government jurisdiction

See Chapter 2 Section 11.2 of your Study Text

19. **A**   The primary market is through the auction by the DMO. The LSE is involved in trading Gilts once they have been issued but is not involved in their original issuance

See Chapter 2 Section 10.3 of your Study Text

20. **D**   A gilt with less than seven years to run is a 'short'. This definition has been created by the DMO

See Chapter 2 Section 10.4 of your Study Text

21. **D**   A Put is the right but not an obligation to sell an asset and a Call is the right but not the obligation to buy an asset. A Forward is a derivative trade done over the counter (OTC): as such, it enables the parties to the trade to tailor the trade to their actual needs. A Future is an agreement to buy or sell a standard quantity of a specified asset on a fixed future date at a price agreed today. That is, a future does not have the flexibility of a forward

See Chapter 1 Section 7.3 and Chapter 3 Sections 2.1 and 3 of your Study Text

22. **A**   Open-Ended Investment Companies (OEICs) are a type of collective investment vehicle whose shares are single-priced. Options B, C and D are incorrect

See Chapter 5 Sections 3.1 and 3.2 of your Study Text

23. **B**   The net amount is the gross less 20% tax on interest. The bank will withhold the 20% at source although if eligible, a customer may reclaim the tax from HMRC by completing an R85 Form. The P11D has nothing to do with interest earned: it concerns benefits from an employer such as medical insurance

See Chapter 4 Section 1 of your Study Text

24. **B**   All other things being equal, a secured loan should have a lower interest rate as there is less risk involved for the bank concerned: as it will have an asset as collateral. An unsecured loan will have no such collateral and therefore the bank is at risk if the borrower defaults. It is for this reason that the bank will charge more than for a secured loan

See Chapter 4 Section 5.3 of your Study Text

25. **D**   One might be tempted to select option A – a loan to purchase a property. While a mortgage is generally a loan to purchase a property, this is a specific use of a mortgage. The best definition of a mortgage however is a secured loan, because a mortgage could be used for things other than property

See Chapter 4 Section 6 of your Study Text

26. **C**   Although a capped mortgage does not have to have a life of five years, all the others have no maximum rate and therefore this answer is the only one that can be correct

See Chapter 4 Section 6.3 of your Study Text

27.   **A**   A whole of life policy will pay out on the death of the life insured and such payments would be included in their estate for IHT purposes. A non-profit whole of life policy has no link to stock market performance and the acceptance or not of an additional life assured is irrelevant. As stated, it is a policy for a fixed sum assured

See Chapter 4 Section 7 of your Study Text

28.   **B**   No charges are allowed in relation to a stakeholder pension transfer

See Chapter 4 Section 3.5 of your Study Text

29.   **C**   Final salary schemes are a form of occupational pension scheme where the employer guarantees to pay a fraction of pre-retirement pay to the retired individual. These are also known as defined benefit schemes

See Chapter 4 Section 3.3.1 of your Study Text

30.   **B**   For new plans, charges are limited to 1.5% of the fund value for the first 10 years and then 1% thereafter. Since you did not have an option showing '1%', there should have been no confusion and 1.5% is the best answer

See Chapter 4 Section 3.5 of your Study Text

31.   **C**   A REIT must distribute at least 90% of its taxable profits if is is to remain exempt from corporation tax

See Chapter 5 Section 7 of your Study Text

32.   **C**   A Depositary in an OEIC is the equivalent of a Trustee in a Unit Trust in that he/she has custody of the assets and serves in an oversight function overseeing the activities of the Authorised Corporate Director who manages the OEIC

See Chapter 5 Section 3.2 of your Study Text

33.   **D**   Two people are required to form a company. Forms must be deposited with the Registrar of Companies for which BIS (the Department for Business, Innovation and Skills) is responsible

See Chapter 2, Section 1.2 of your Study Text

34.   **A**   An investment trust is a company like any other plc, except that its business is investing in other companies. As a company, its shares are traded on the stock market and hence its shares may be bought via a stock broker

See Chapter 5 Section 4.1 and 4.2 of your Study Text

35.   **C**   As a company trading on the Stock Exchange, an investment trust is set up like any other public company with a certain amount of authorised and issued capital and shares. 'Closed-ended' refers to a limited number of shares in issue. It is known as 'closed end' since its authorised and issued capital can only be altered via changes to its memorandum of Association. An 'open ended' fund can vary its capital at will

See Chapter 5 Section 4.1 of your Study Text

36.   **C**   The maximum amount that can be invested in a cash ISA is £5,100 in 2010/11 – irrespective of age

See Chapter 6 Section 1.2 of your Study Text

37. **C** 'UCITS' stands for Undertakings for Collective Investments in Transferable Securities

    See Chapter 5 Section 2.9 of your Study Text

38. **D** Answers A, B and C are statutory objectives of FSMA 2000. The fourth objective is the reduction of financial crime, which encompasses the prevention of money laundering although it is not a specific objective itself

    See Chapter 7 Section 2.2 of your Study Text

39. **B** The firm should make clear that an employee with suspicions should pass such suspicions on to the MLRO. The MLRO is the conduit through which an FSA-authorised firm reports suspicious transactions to SOCA

    See Chapter 7 Sections 3.5.1 and 3.5.2 of your Study Text

40. **B** Interest received on a bond is the coupon. Dividends are paid on shares. A debenture is a type of corporate bond. The yield is a measure of relative return

    See Chapter 2 Section 10.1 of your Study Text

41. **C** If an FSA-authorised firm receives a complaint and it does not get resolved within 24 hours then, as part of its final response, which must be made no later than eight weeks from the complaint being received, it must advise the client of his/her right to refer his/her complaint to the Financial Ombudsman Service. The client then has a maximum of six months to do so for the complaint to receive attention from FOS

    See Chapter 7 Section 6.1.1 of your Study Text

42. **C** A family may invest up to £1,200 per year in a Child Trust Fund for each separate child

    See Chapter 6 Section 2 of your Study Text

43. **A** Since an OEIC is involved in carrying out regulated activities, such as dealing in shares, it must be authorised and regulated by the FSA in accordance with s19 of FSMA 2000

    See Chapter 5 Section 3.3 of your Study Text

44. **C** Term assurance normally has no surrender or maturity value. Whole of life policies will pay out regardless of when death occurs. Unit-linked policies have a direct link with the performance of the underlying fund, the value of which may fluctuate

    See Chapter 4, Section 7 of your Study Text

45. **A** B, C and D would certainly attract the attention of the FSA and may result in fines being imposed against a firm. However, a claim can only be made under the FSCS when a firm fails

    See Chapter 7 Section 6.3 of your Study Text

46. **B** The CAC index relates to France (Paris); The Nikkei relates to Japan (Tokyo) and the Mibtel relates to Italy (Milan). The index for the stock market of Germany is indeed the Dax

    See Chapter 2 Section 6.2 of your Study Text

47. **C** If the rate is 8% payable quarterly then you will pay 2% each quarter. To calculate the Annual Equivalent Rate you must take 1.02 to the power 4, subtract 1 and multiply the result by 100. This comes to $(1.0824 - 1) \times 100 = 0.0824 \times 100 = 8.24$

   See Chapter 4 Section 5.2 of your Study Text

48. **B** Answers C and D are unrelated to the activities of market makers. Answer A is also incorrect because simply Market Makers are not forecasting prices but quoting prices and sizes of transactions at which they will deal, which is why answer B is correct

   See Chapter 2 Section 8.1 of your Study Text

49. **B** Answers C and D are 'red herrings' and are incorrect. Answer A can have an effect on equivalent rates but this question refers to a simple interest quotation for a loan and it is convention that unless otherwise stated, it would be on an annual basis. The effective rate of interest on the loan will be the same as the simple rate providing that the interest is only paid once per year. If more often then the effective rate will be higher. This is why the correct answer is B

   See Chapter 4 Sections 5.1 and 5.2 of your Study Text

50. **C** The amount is calculated as 100% of the first £50,000

   See Chapter 7, Section 6.3 of your Study Text

Practice Examination 3

50 Questions in 1 Hour

1. Which of the following has the primary purpose of raising finance for businesses?

   A   Hedge fund

   B   Securities house

   C   Investment bank

   D   Bank of England

2. A currency transaction normally settles

   A   T + 1

   B   T + 2

   C   T + 3

   D   T + 5

3. An investor owns £8,000 of Treasury 8% 2012 trading at a market price of £106. What is the flat yield?

   A   7.5%

   B   6.0%

   C   8.0%

   D   6.5%

4. What is the normal effect of credit creation?

   A   Increase in money supply

   B   Increase in balance of payments deficit

   C   Decrease in inflation

   D   Increase in unemployment

5. Which is the measure used to determine the level of imports and exports?

   A   Retail Prices Index

   B   Base rate

   C   Public Sector Net Cash Requirement

   D   Balance of payments

6. ✓ **Which of the following is a function of the Bank of England?**

   A Issue gilts on behalf of the Treasury

   B Regulate retail banks

   Ⓒ Monitor the value of sterling and intervene in currency markets

   D Set the terms of National Savings & Investments products

7. ✓ **Which of the following is an example of wholesale insurance?**

   A Critical illness

   Ⓑ Risk-sharing

   C Income replacement

   D Mortgage protection

8. ✗ **What would be the most likely effect of an increase in the PSNCR?**

   A Higher unemployment

   Ⓑ Reduction in balance of payments deficit

   C Reduction in GDP

   D̲ Increase in inflation

9. ✓ **Which of the following is a reason to invest in a fixed term deposit rather than an 'instant access' account?**

   A Benefit from a higher level of protection from the Financial Services Compensation Scheme

   B Maximisation of tax benefits

   Ⓒ Benefit from a higher rate of interest

   D Lower risk of default

10. ✓ **Which type of market are money market instruments generally considered to service?**

   Ⓐ Short-term wholesale cash market

   B Long-term wholesale cash market

   C Short-term retail cash market

   D Long-term retail cash market

11. ✗ **In which of the following types of property is an institutional investor least likely to invest?**

   A̲ Residential property

   B Small commercial property

   Ⓒ Industrial property

   D Farmland property

12. Which of the following is an index for the stock market of France?

    Ⓐ CAC 40

    B Mibtel

    C Nikkei 225

    D Dax

13. Which of the following is a restriction placed on private limited companies?

    A Any sale of the company must be approved by Companies House.

    B Shares may not be sold in blocks of more than 1000 shares.

    Ⓒ Shares may not be issued to the public.

    D Any sale of the company must be approved by 75% of shareholders.

14. What percentage of a company's shares should be in public hands in order to meet the requirements of a 'full listing' under UKLA rules?

    A 10%

    B 20%

    Ⓒ 25%

    D 33.3%

15. The Alternative Investment Market exists mainly to allow investment in

    A Large multinational companies

    Ⓑ Smaller, growing companies

    C UK large companies

    D Derivatives

16. An ordinary shareholder has the right to

    A Be paid a dividend

    Ⓑ Vote on the appointment of a director

    C A return of capital on liquidation

    D Call for an extraordinary general meeting

17. An issue of free new shares to an existing shareholder in proportion to their existing holding, as at the record date, is known as a

    Ⓐ Bonus issue

    B Scrip dividend

    C Rights issue

    D Return of capital

18. SETS is available for trading in

A   All PLUS shares

B   Only FTSE 350 shares

C   All AIM shares

(D)   All FTSE 100 shares

19. Which of the following measures is used to determine whether a company's shares are included in the FTSE 100 Index?

(A)   Market capitalisation

B   Net profit after tax

C   Turnover

D   Size of the workforce

20. Which of the following is the primary criterion for determining the legal title of a share?

A   Possession of a share certificate

(B)   Entry on register

C   Records of electronic holdings held by CREST (Euroclear UK & Ireland)

D   Contract note with details of trade

21. A sells shares to B and the transaction takes place through CREST (Euroclear UK & Ireland or EUI). How will the registrar be informed of the change of ownership in order to make the necessary amendments?

A   A's bank will inform the registrar

(B)   B's bank will inform the registrar

C   CREST (EUI) will send an electronic message to the registrar

D   CREST (EUI) will send a share certificate and stock transfer form to the Registrar

22. The primary purpose of issuing gilts is to

A   To raise money for business

B   To fund government borrowing

(C)   To reduce the balance of payments

D   To reduce the National Debt

23. A gilt with five years left before maturity is know as a

A   Long

B   Medium

(C)   Short

D   Repo

24. ⤫ **A bond has a coupon of 7.5%. What will the price of the bond be if general interest rates are 6%?**

   A   £80.00

   Ⓑ   £101.50

   C   £115.00

   D   £125.00

25. ✓ **Which of the following is the best definition of a future?**

   A   A flexible contract where the investor buys and asset and agrees to sell it a future date

   B   A flexible contract where the value is based on price movements of an underlying asset

   C   A standardised contract where the holder has the right to buy an asset before an expiry date

   Ⓓ   A standardised contract where the holder agrees to buy or sell a specified issue at a specified price on a specified date

26. ⤫ **An investor who has 'opened a short position'**

   A   Is committed to buying the underlying asset at a pre-agreed price on a future date

   B   Is committed to selling the underlying asset at a pre-agreed price on a future date

   C   Has the right but not an obligation to buy the underlying asset at a pre-agreed price on a future date

   Ⓓ   Has the right but not an obligation to sell the underlying asset at a pre-agreed price on a future date

27. ✓ **Which is the best definition of an interest rate swap?**

   A   An agreement that is sometimes known as a Contract for Discount

   B   An agreement whereby a fixed interest payment is always swapped with LIBOR + 25 basis points

   Ⓒ   An agreement to exchange, over an agreed period, payment streams based on different types of interest rates, but which are based on the same notional principal amount

   D   An agreement which gives the investor the option of swapping a fixed rate for a floating rate

28. ⤫ **Which of the following is carried out by the manager of a unit trust?**

   A   Pricing

   Ⓑ   Safeguarding assets

   C   Protecting the interests of investors

   D   Creating and cancelling units

29. ✓ **Which of the following would normally sell units in a unit trust?**

    A   Registrar

    B   Trustee

    Ⓒ   Manager

    D   Depository

30. ✗ **Which of the following is the independent overseer of the board of an OEIC?**

    A   Trustee

    Ⓑ   FSA

    C   Depository

    D   ACD

31. ✗ **How is the price of an OEIC share set?**

    A   Bid price of underlying investments

    Ⓑ   Offer price of underlying investments

    C   Mid-price of underlying investments

    D   Estimated fair value of investments

32. ✓ **What is meant by the term 'closed-ended' in relation to an investment trust?**

    A   Fund has a limited life

    Ⓑ   Share capital is fixed

    C   Only institutional investors may purchase the fund

    D   The fund invests in a fixed set of investments

33. ✓ **What is the meaning of 'trading at a premium' in relation to an investment trust?**

    Ⓐ   Share price is above net asset value

    B   Share price is below net asset value

    C   Price is based on NAV with charges added

    D   Price is based on NAV with charges deducted

34. ✗ **Which investment would allow an investor to have an exposure to an ungeared fund investing in FTSE 100 stocks with a very narrow bid-offer spread and real-time pricing?**

    A   An at-the-money FTSE 100 call option

    B   An out-of-the-money FTSE 100 call option

    C   A FTSE 100 exchange traded fund

    Ⓓ   A FTSE 100 tracker unit trust

35. Which of the following is a fund often with an aggressive investment strategy taking advantage of arbitrage, short positions, futures and options and swaps?

A Hedge fund

B Equity fund

C Fixed interest fund

D Exchange traded fund

36. In which of the following does the FSA have an objective to maintain confidence?

A UK financial system

B European financial system

C UK financial firms

D European financial firms

37. Which of the following are the three stages of money laundering?

A Inception, layering, separation

B Initiation, integration, withdrawal

C Placement, layering, integration

D Inception, separation, withdrawal

38. Which of the following would not normally be satisfactory evidence of the identity of an individual for money laundering purposes?

A Photographic driving licence

B Electoral roll entry

C Recent utility bill

D National Insurance number

39. Which of the following would be considered to be insider dealing?

A A director dealing on non-public price sensitive information

B A director dealing during the three months prior to publication of the accounts

C A director dealing in the shares of an associate company

D A director dealing in any closed period for the shares where this is part of a regular commitment to purchase

40. Which of the following is a principal objective of the Data Protection Act?

A To ensure that information on individuals is kept for no longer than one year

B To ensure that companies do not release price sensitive information

C To ensure that information on individuals is accurate and up to date

D To ensure that the correct information is included in the financial statements of the company concerned

41. A financial adviser has received a written complaint from a client. He deals with the complaint and advises the client that he/she can refer the matter to the Financial Ombudsman Service (FOS) if he/she is unsatisfied with the response. How much time does the complainant have to refer the matter to FOS?

    A Five working days

    B Four weeks

    C Eight weeks

    D Six months

42. How much would an investor receive from the Financial Services Compensation Scheme if he incurred a loss of £65,000 in investments following the insolvency of an FSA authorised firm?

    A £48,000

    B £50,000

    C £61,500

    D £65,000

43. How old must an investor be to open a stocks and shares ISA?

    A 15

    B 16

    C 17

    D 18

44. What normally happens to a Child Trust Fund when the child reaches the age of 13?

    A The fund is no longer wholly tax-free

    B The charging structure is reviewed

    C The investments may be gradually moved into lower risk funds

    D The child is given more control over the account

45. What is the maximum charge under a newly opened stakeholder pension plan?

    A 1% of bid/offer spread

    B £1 per month

    C 1.5% of fund value

    D £100 per annum

46. Which of the following will be subject to CGT on disposal?

    A Gilts

    B Principal residence

    C Car

    D Options

47. Which of the following will not be subject to income tax?

A Dividend income

B Sale of shares

C Interest on bonds

D Interest on bank accounts

48. Who is the legal owner of assets in a trust?

A Settlor

B Trustee

C Beneficiary

D Remaindermen

49. What kind of mortgage is an ISA mortgage?

A Lifetime

B Repayment

C Interest-only

D Pension linked

50. What type of policy is a whole of life policy which has a sum assured of £120,000 throughout the term of the policy?

A Non-profit

B Traditional with-profit

C Unitised with-profit

D Unit-linked

Answers

1. **C**   An investment bank has the primary purpose of raising finance for businesses. Securities houses do this amongst many other functions

See Chapter 1 Section 3.3 of your Study Text

2. **B**   Spot currency trades settle T + 2

See Chapter 1 Section 7.2 of your Study Text

3. **A**   The flat yield is calculated as follows

$$\text{Flat yield} = \frac{\text{Gross coupon}}{\text{Market price}} \times 100$$

$$= \frac{£8}{£106} \times 100$$

$$= 7.5\%$$

See Chapter 2, Section 11.7 of your Study Text

4. **A**   Credit creation increases the money supply

See Chapter 1 Section 1.7 of your Study Text

5. **D**   Balance of payments is a measure of imports and exports

See Chapter1 Section 1.9.3 of your Study Text

6. **C**   The Monetary Policy Committee of the Bank of England sets the repo rate. The Bank does not directly set the terms of NS&I products. The Bank can intervene in the currency markets to influence the value of sterling

See Chapter 1 Section 2.1 of your Study Text

7. **B**   Risk-sharing insurance is wholesale, the others are forms of retail insurance bought by retail clients

See Chapter 1 Sections 3.7 and 8.2 of your Study Text

8. **D**   Increase in inflation is the most likely effect of an increase in PSNCR since the government, via the DMO, issues gilts to fund the PSNCR and then the money borrowed money leads to increased money supply and inflation

See Chapter 1 Section 1.8 and Chapter 2 Section 10.3 of your Study Text

9. **C**   Interest rates tend to be higher on fixed term deposits rather than instant access

See Chapter 4 Section 1 of your Study Text

10. **A**   Money market instruments are generally seen to service the short-term wholesale cash market

See Chapter 2 Section 12.1 of your Study Text

11. **A**   Most institutional investors avoid residential property, although there are some funds that specialise in this area

See Chapter 4 Section 2.1 of your Study Text

12. **A**   CAC 40 is the main French index

See Chapter 2 Section 6.2 of your Study Text

13. **C**   Shares in private companies may not be sold to the public

See Chapter 2 Section 1.2 of your Study Text

14. **C**   25% of shares need to be in public hands

See Chapter 2 Section 4.3 of your Study Text

15. **B**   Smaller, growing companies tend to list on AIM

See Chapter 2 Section 5 of your Study Text

16. **B**   An ordinary shareholder will have the right to vote on appointment of a director and may benefit from the other options

See Chapter 2 Section 2.1.1 of your Study Text

17. **A**   Free shares *pro rata* to the existing holding comprises a bonus issue

See Chapter 2 Section 3.2 of your Study Text

18. **D**   All FTSE 100 shares are quoted on SETS as are all FTSE 350 shares. However, the key word here is 'only' which makes the phrase 'only FTSE 350 shares' an incorrect statement

See Chapter 2 Section 7.1 of your Study Text

19. **A**   Market capitalisation is the qualifying criterion for entry into FTSE 100

See Chapter 2 Section 6.2 of your Study Text

20. **B**   Entry on the company register of shareholders is used to determine legal title to shares

See Chapter 2 Section 9.4.6 of your Study Text

21. **C**   CREST (Euroclear UK & Ireland) will send an RUR (Register Update Request) to the registrar to initiate the update of the register

See Chapter 2 Section 9.6 of your Study Text

22. **B**   Gilts are a method used to fund government borrowing

See Chapter 2 Section 10.1 of your Study Text

23. **C**   Shorts are any gilt with a remaining time to maturity of less than 7 years (according to DMO definitions)

See Chapter 2 Section 10.4 of your Study Text

24. **D**   Coupon is higher than general interest rates so the bond will be priced above par (above £100). At a price of £125 the yield is 6% which is the same as the general rate

See Chapter 2 Section 11.7 of your Study Text

25. **D** Futures are standardised and have a specified date and price

See Chapter 3 Section 2.1 of your Study Text

26. **B** A short position is a commitment to sell

See Chapter 3 Section 2.2 of your Study Text

27. **C** An interest rate swap (IRS) is defined as an agreement to exchange, over an agreed period, two payment streams each calculated using a different type of interest rate. (The payments are also based upon the same notional principal amount)

See Chapter 3 Section 5 of your Study Text

28. **A** Pricing is carried out by the fund manager

See Chapter 5 Section 2.1 of your Study Text

29. **C** The manager ensures that there is a market by buying and selling the units

See Chapter 5 Section 2.1 of your Study Text

30. **C** The depository is the independent overseer of the OEIC's board

See Chapter 5 Section 3.2 of your Study Text

31. **C** OEICs are most commonly single-priced, based on the mid-value of the underlying investments

See Chapter 5 Section 3.2 of your Study Text

32. **B** Share capital is fixed

See Chapter 5 Section 4.1 of your Study Text

33. **A** Share price is above NAV due to increased demand for the fund

See Chapter 5 Section 4.2 of your Study Text

34. **C** The answer cannot refer to options since they are geared – ie in this case permitting the magnification of profits or losses in relation to the investment of the premium. The narrow bid-offer spread indicates an exchange traded fund rather than a unit trust

See Chapter 5 Section 5 of your Study Text

35. **A** Hedge funds tend to use the investment strategies mentioned in the question

See Chapter 5 Section 6 of your Study Text

36. **A** It is an objective of the FSA to maintain confidence in the UK financial system

See Chapter 7 Section 2.1 of your Study Text

37. **C** Placement, layering and integration are the three stages of money laundering

See Chapter 7 Section 3.2 of your Study Text

38. **D** National Insurance number is not proof of identity

See Chapter 7 Section 3.8 of your Study Text

39. **A** Dealing on non-public price sensitive information is the definition of insider dealing

    See Chapter 7 Section 4.2 of your Study Text

40. **C** Information must be kept accurate and up to date

    See Chapter 7 Section 5 of your Study Text

41. **D** A complainant must refer the matter to FOS within six months otherwise he/she risks that the matter will not be dealt with

    See Chapter 7 Section 6.1.1 of your Study Text

42. **B** 100% x £50,000 = £50,000

    See Chapter 7 Section 6.3 of your Study Text

43. **D** An investor must be aged at least 18 (and UK-resident) to open a stocks and shares ISA (although the limit is age 16 or over for a cash ISA)

    See Chapter 6 Section 1.1 of your Study Text

44. **C** The investments can be gradually moved into lower risk funds

    See Chapter 6 Section 2 of your Study Text

45. **C** 1.5% is currently the maximum charge on a newly opened stakeholder pension plan

    See Chapter 4 Section 3.5 of your Study Text

46. **D** If an asset does not have a specific exemption then it is chargeable to CGT. Options would be subject to CGT whereas the other choices are all exempt

    See Chapter 8 Section 2.2 of your Study Text

47. **B** The sale of shares is potentially liable to CGT. All the others are forms of income and hence subject to Income Tax

    See Chapter 8 Sections 1 and 2 of your Study Text

48. **B** The trustee is the legal owner of assets in the trust

    See Chapter 8 Section 8.2 of your Study Text

49. **C** An ISA mortgage is an interest-only mortgage since it is independent of the mortgage itself upon which interest is paid

    See Chapter 4 Section 6.2 and Chapter 6 Sections 1.1 and 1.2 of your Study Text

50. **A** Non-profit policies have a fixed sum assured

    See Chapter 4 Section 7 of your Study Text

Practice Examination 4

50 Questions in 1 Hour

1. What does the S&P 500 index represent?

   (A) A broad view of the US equity market

   B A narrow view of the US equity market

   C A broad view of the US commodity market

   D A narrow view of the US commodity market

2. Fixed interest securities usually entitle the owner to

   (A) Regular interest payments

   B A vote at the AGM of the issuing company

   C A right to dividend payments

   D Repayment of the price paid for the security

3. Which of the following is covered by the Companies Act 2006?

   A Insider dealing

   (B) Listing rules

   C Money laundering

   D Protection of shareholders from abuses of power by directors

4. A taxpayer would not pay income tax in respect of which of the following?

   A Dividends

   (B) Sale of shares

   C Bond interest

   D Bank and building society interest

5. What is the name of the instrument that gives the buyer the right, but not the obligation, to buy the underlying equity at some time in the future?

   A A future

   (B) A call

   C A forward

   D A put

6. × **What is the effect on the value of an investor's portfolio of a bonus issue?**

   Ⓐ The portfolio will fall in value

   B The portfolio will rise in value

   C̲ The portfolio will be unchanged

   D Indeterminate

7. ✓ **Which of the following statements best describes a rights issue?**

   A A free issue of shares to existing shareholders in proportion to their existing holding

   Ⓑ An issue of shares to existing shareholders in proportion to their existing holding at a predetermined price

   C An issue of shares to existing shareholders in proportion to their existing holding at the current market price

   D An issue of shares to the market at a predetermined price

8. ✓ **Which of the following statements regarding indices is false?**

   Ⓐ The Dow Jones Industrial Average represents 33 top US companies

   B The Nikkei Dow represents 225 Japanese companies

   C The DAX represents the 30 leading German companies

   D Investors use indices for benchmarking purposes

9. ✓ **After 5 April 2010, the earliest age at which a pension-linked mortgage can normally be repaid using the pension plan proceeds is**

   A 50

   Ⓑ 55

   C 60

   D 65

10. ✓ **The FTSE 250 index covers**

    A The 250 best performing companies in the UK

    B The largest 250 companies listed on the LSE weighted by market capitalisation

    Ⓒ The next 250 companies listed on the LSE weighted by market capitalisation after the companies in the FTSE 100

    D The full list of AIM companies

11. ✓ **In the UK, equity trades settle on which of the following bases?**

    A T + 1

    B T + 2

    Ⓒ T + 3

    D T + 4

12. Which of the following investments would not have capital gains tax applied to a trading gain when sold?

A Gold

B Gilts

C Stamp collection

D Shares

13. Which of the following is a 'closed-ended' investment?

A Unit trusts

B Investment trusts

C OEICs

D Unit trust ISAs

14. Which of the following are quoted companies that are set up for the purpose of investing in the shares of other companies?

A Unit trusts

B Investment trusts

C OEICs

D Unit trust ISAs

15. The date shown on a share certificate will be

A The trade date

B The settlement date

C The date of transfer effected by the registrar

D Two weeks after trade date

16. When will a foreign exchange deal struck on Monday normally settle?

A Tuesday

B Wednesday

C Thursday

D Friday

17. If a developed economy displays a high level of inflation, which of the following is the most likely result?

A Certainty as to the value of personal investments

B Balance of payments surplus

C Loss of international competitiveness

D Higher taxation

18. **Which of the following is the best definition of money laundering?**

    A   Making shareholder profits by using information not in the public domain

    (B) The process by which criminals attempt to hide the true origin of the proceeds of criminal activities

    C   Trading in multiple small parcels of shares to disguise the purchase of a holding in excess of 3%

    D   Directors trading in the shares of a company within one month of the publication of company results

19. **What is another commonly used name for equity?**

    A   Gilts

    B   Warrants

    (C) Shares

    D   Futures

20. **Which of the following would not be a reason for owning a gilt?**

    A   To receive regular interest income payments

    B   A guaranteed redemption value

    C   To achieve better diversification of a portfolio

    (D) To gain more interest income as general interest rates rise

21. **What is the term used when describing the fixed income return earned when investing in a bond?**

    A   Dividend

    B   Yield

    (C) Coupon

    D   Return

22. **Which of the following indices represents almost all of the relevant country's market capitalisation?**

    (A) FTSE All Share

    B   FTSE 100

    C   S&P 500

    D   Nikkei 225

23. Which of the following would most likely be the reason to own shares instead of fixed income instruments?

   A   To receiving voting rights and guaranteed, regular income
   B   To receive guaranteed, regular income and a redemption value after ten years
   C   To receiving voting rights and potential capital appreciation
   D   To receiving guaranteed, regular income and the right of first refusal to new shares in the company

24. For unit trusts, which of the following are duties of the investment manager?

   I   Safeguarding the assets
   II   Investing the assets
   III   Pricing the assets
   IV   Being the legal owner of the assets

   A   I and II
   B   I, II and III
   C   II and IV
   D   II and III

25. Which of the following roles would most likely be performed by an LSE member firm?

   A   Funds management
   B   Market making
   C   Mergers and acquisitions
   D   Futures trading

26. Which of the following is the most likely role for an investment bank to fulfil?

   A   Credit provision
   B   Mergers and acquisitions
   C   Global custody
   D   Stock lending

27. Calculate the total net interest payment received by a higher rate taxpayer who deposits £10,000 in a bank account yielding 5% per annum over four years.

   A   £400
   B   £500
   C   £1,600
   D   £2,000

28. Which of the following is one of the four statutory objectives of the FSA?

    (A) Maintaining confidence in the UK financial system

    B Maintaining confidence in the European financial system

    C Maintaining confidence in UK financial companies

    D Maintaining confidence in European financial companies

29. Which of the following is not a type of a unit trust?

    A UCITS fund

    B A non-retail UCITS retail scheme

    C A qualified investor scheme

    (D) Exchange-traded funds

30. Which of the following organises the issuance of UK government bonds?

    A The Bank of England

    B London Stock Exchange

    (C) Debt Management Office

    D NYSE Liffe

31. Which one of the following types of risk does not contribute to credit risk?

    A Interest rate risk

    B Issuer risk

    C Counterparty risk

    (D) Settlement risk

32. Which of the following statements is true with regard to the Financial Services Compensation Scheme (FSCS)?

    (A) The FSCS will adjudicate in a dispute between an eligible claimant and an FSA-authorised firm

    B Directors of failed FSA-authorised firms who hold cash deposit accounts are not eligible to claim under the FSCS

    C The FSCS is accountable to the FSA and HM Treasury

    D Under the FSCS, the maximum award for deposits is £35,000

33. Which of the following is a benefit of a company being quoted on the LSE? (Choose the most appropriate answer.)

    A The ability to pay dividends annually

    B The requirement to report on a regular basis

    (C) The ability to use newly issued shares to purchase the shares of companies being taken over

    D The ability to market products

34. ✗ **Which of the following types of organisation is involved in credit creation?**

Ⓐ Central banks

B Insurance companies

C Commercial banks

D Stock brokers

35. ✓ **Which of the following is not a function of the Bank of England?**

A Provision of economic statistics

B Setting interest rates

Ⓒ Banking supervision

D Control of the amount of notes and coins in circulation

36. ✗ **You place an order with SETS to sell 80,000 shares at £3.64, but there are only bids for 50,000 shares. If the remainder of the order remains on SETS, which one of the following orders would it be?**

A Market order

B Fill or kill order

Ⓒ Execute and eliminate order

D Limit order

37. ✓ **Which trading platform would you probably be using for trading a share that has low liquidity?**

A SETS

Ⓑ SETSqx

C CoredealMTS

D CREST (Euroclear UK & Ireland)

38. ✓ **Which one of the following would mean that the offence of insider dealing has been committed?**

A Dealing without the intention of making a profit

B Dealing on information you believed was generally available

C Dealing, despite the information known, in order to settle a debt

Ⓓ Dealing on information that is not available to the general public

39. ✗ **What is the maximum lifespan of a Commercial Paper?**

A 30 days

Ⓑ 90 days

C 180 days

D 365 days

40. ✓ **Which of the following exchanges acquired Euronext?**

    A   Börse

    B   OM Gruppen

    C   NASDAQ

    (D) NYSE

41. ✓ **Which of the following are true of market abuse?**

    I   It is a civil offence
    II   The maximum sentence if found guilty is seven years in jail and an unlimited fine
    III   It relates to trading based on unavailable information
    IV   It relates to trading on RIEs and PLUS

    A   I, II, III and IV

    B   I and IV

    C   I, II and IV

    (D) I, III and IV

42. ✓ **Which of the following is the reason for the issuance of gilts?**

    A   To ensure that there is a strong cash flow within the UK economy

    B   To provide investors with a higher return when interest rates are low

    (C) To fund government spending in excess of receipts

    D   To ensure that there is a high level of central reserves

43. ✓ **Which of the following is regarded as a function of the Bank of England?**

    A   To provide regulation of the banking sector

    B   To provide personal customers with accounts

    C   To issue gilts

    (D) To control the amount of notes and coins in circulation

44. ✓ **A bullish investor opening a position in the June FTSE future is described as being**

    (A) Long

    B   Short

    C   Flat

    D   In the money

45. ✓ **Which of the following is the best description with regard to GDP?**

    A   It represents the value of all activities paid for in cash and other financial activities

    (B) It is the goods and services produced within an economy

    C   A rising GDP will indicate a falling standard of living

    D   It will include black market activity

46. With respect to fund managers, which of the following statements is true?

A   Fund management relates to activities concerned with advice and corporate action processing on behalf of investors

B   Fund management may be done individually or collectively, the latter being the more expensive option of the two

C   Fund management decisions must not only match the needs of the client, but also diversify away risk

D   Fund management is an activity frequently performed by investment banks

47. Which of the following is the nil rate band for inheritance tax for the fiscal year 2010/2011?

A   £125,000

B   £300,000

C   £325,000

D   £500,000

48. Which of the following is the best description of a takeover?

A   The management buying out the shareholders of a company

B   One company buying out another company

C   The liquidation of a company

D   Shareholders voting to remove the Chief Executive of a company

49. Where is the main legislation regarding market abuse to be found?

A   FSMA 2000

B   UKLA Listing Rules

C   Criminal Justice Act 1993

D   Proceeds of Crime Act 2002

50. Which of the following is the best definition of insider trading?

A   Making profits from share trading by using information not in the public domain

B   The process by which criminals attempt to hide the true origin of the proceeds of criminal activities

C   Trading in multiple small packets of shares to disguise the purchase of a holding in excess of 3%

D   Directors trading in the shares of a company within one month of the publication of company results

Answers

1. **A** The S&P 500 is broader than the Dow Jones Industrial Average, which only covers 30 US shares

    See Chapter 2, Section 6.2 of your Study Text

2. **A** It is shareholders who have the right to vote and receive dividends, if the company pays them. Fixed interest securities will entitle the bondholder to nominal value on redemption

    See Chapter 2, Sections 10.1 and 11.1 of your Study Text

3. **D** Insider trading, listing and money laundering are each covered by specific legislation

    See Chapter 2, Section 1.1 of your Study Text

4. **B** Dividends, bond interest and bank and building society interest are all subject to income tax. Profits on sale of shares are subject to capital gains tax

    See Chapter 8, Sections 1 and 2 of your Study Text

5. **B** The right to buy is a 'call', an obligation to buy would be a long future

    See Chapter 3, Section 3.1 of your Study Text

6. **C** Remember that a bonus issue is used by companies to improve liquidity by spreading the value of the company among a greater number of shares. Existing shareholders are given new shares, completely free. Thus, while the individual share price will be lower, the portfolio still has the same overall value

    See Chapter 2, Section 3.2 of your Study Text

7. **B** Existing shareholders have pre-emption rights (a right of first refusal), allowing them to take up the offer and purchase new shares at the predetermined subscription price

    See Chapter 2, Section 3.3 of your Study Text

8. **A** The Dow Jones represents the top 30 US companies

    See Chapter 2, Section 6.2 of your Study Text

9. **B** Repayment of the mortgage is made from the tax-free cash paid on retirement out of a pension plan. Pension benefits may be taken between 55 and 75 years of age under HMRC rules. (The lower age limit was 50 before 6 April 2010)

    See Chapter 4, Section 3.4 of your Study Text

10. **C** The FTSE 250 Index comprises the shares of the 250 largest companies after the top 100 companies listed on the LSE

    See Chapter 2, Section 6.2 of your Study Text

11. **C** T + 3

    See Chapter 2, Section 9.2 of your Study Text

12. **B** Gilts are exempt from CGT

    See Chapter 8, Section 2.2 of your Study Text

13. **B** Investment trusts close for subscription after their launch. Their value then tracks the value of the funds invested

See Chapter 5, Section 4.1 of your Study Text

14. **B** Investment trusts are quoted companies priced on the LSE

See Chapter 5, Section 4.1 of your Study Text

15. **C** It is only when the registrar has amended the share register that the buyer of the shares becomes the new legal owner and enjoys all the rights and privileges that accompany being a shareholder

See Chapter 2, Section 2.3 of your Study Text

16. **B** Spot forex transactions normally settle T + 2, so a deal struck on Monday will settle on Wednesday, i.e. a three-day period. This is a tricky question since it does not specify whether we are dealing with spot or forward trades

See Chapter 1, Section 7.2 of your Study Text

17. **C** This is the best answer available. There are many other consequences of inflation, including the erosion of the value of personal investments

See Chapter 1, Section 1.8 of your Study Text

18. **B** This is a good definition of money laundering

See Chapter 7, Section 3.1 of your Study Text

19. **C** Shares are also known as equity investments

See Chapter 2, Section 1.5 of your Study Text

20. **D** When the Debt Management Office issues a gilt, the coupon (which determines the amount of interest income that will be received) is fixed. Only a floating rate instrument will offer additional interest income if general interest rates rise

See Chapter 2, Section 10.2 of your Study Text

21. **C** Dividend for equities, coupons for bonds

See Chapter 2, Section 10.1 of your Study Text

22. **A** The FTSE 100 is an index of the top 100 shares by market capitalisation, while the FTSE All Share is an index of all listed companies. The FTSE All Share represents approximately 98% of the UK market by value

See Chapter 2, Section 6.2 of your Study Text

23. **C** Ordinary shares carry voting rights but no legal right to a dividend. However, ordinary shareholders will share equally in a dividend, should one be declared by a company

See Chapter 2, Section 2.1 of your Study Text

24. **D** The investment manager is responsible for trading the assets and pricing the units. The trustee looks after the issuance of new units and is the legal owner of the assets

See Chapter 5, Section 2.1 of your Study Text

25. **B** This is the best answer available, as some LSE members also manage funds. The key point to note is that you cannot be a market maker without being an LSE member, whereas fund managers do not have to be LSE members

See Chapter 1, Sections 3.8 and 4.1 of your Study Text

26. **B** Investment banks tend not to provide credit. Custody and stocklending is the role of the global custodian

See Chapter 1, Section 3.3 of your Study Text

27. **C** The total net Interest payment may be calculated as follows

£10,000 × 5% = £500 per annum, thus £2,000 over the four years

Remember that banks and building societies will deduct 20% withholding tax (or the basic rate of tax on interest income) at source. Thus

£2,000 × (1 – Tax rate) = £1,600

Further, the investor will be liable to pay a further 20%

See Chapter 4, Section 1 of your Study Text

28. **A** The FSA has the task of maintaining confidence in the UK financial system. The other statutory objectives are public awareness, reduction of financial crime and protection of consumers

See Chapter 7, Section 2.2 of your Study Text

29. **D** Unit trusts are not exchange-traded; units are traded via the fund manager

See Chapter 5, Section 2.3 of your Study Text

30. **C** The Debt Management Office is the full name. The DMO is an agency of the Treasury

See Chapter 2, Section 10.3 of your Study Text

31. **A** Issuer risk, counterparty risk and settlement risk are all components of credit risk

See Chapter 2, Section 2.2 of your Study Text

32. **C** Following August 2009 rule changes, directors of the failed entity are entitled to compensation, in respect of deposits. The Financial Ombudsman Service is the body responsible for adjudication of disputes

See Chapter 7, Section 6.3 of your Study Text

33. **C** The only definite advantage is the ability to use shares to finance the takeover of target companies

See Chapter 2, Section 4.1 of your Study Text

34. **C** The creation of credit can be achieved by the 'recycling' of funds placed on deposit with banks

See Chapter 1, Section 1.7 of your Study Text

35. **C** Since the Bank of England Act 1998, this responsibility has passed to the FSA

See Chapter 1, Section 2.1 of your Study Text

36. **D** Only a limit order will leave an unexecuted part on the order book if not fully completed

See Chapter 2, Section 7.3 of your Study Text

37. **B** Liquid shares trade on SETS. CREST (Euroclear UK & Ireland) is a settlement house, not a trading platform

See Chapter 2, Section 8.2 of your Study Text

38. **D** Insider dealing is trading on information that is not publicly available

See Chapter 7, Section 4.2 of your Study Text

39. **D** Commercial paper has a lifespan of between eight and 365 days

See Chapter 2, Section 12.2 of your Study Text

40. **D** NYSE purchased Euronext to create the merged entity NYSE Euronext

See Chapter 1, Section 6.2 of your Study Text

41. **D** Since this is a civil offence, the guilty party cannot be sent to jail

See Chapter 7, Section 4.3 of your Study Text

42. **C** Gilts are issued to finance the spending of the Government in excess of tax revenues achieved

See Chapter 1, Section 1.9.3 of your Study Text

43. **D** The Bank controls the amount of notes and coins in circulation. The DMO issues gilts. The FSA now regulates the banking sector

See Chapter 1, Section 2.1 of your Study Text

44. **A** A transaction in which a future is purchased to open a position is known as a long position

See Chapter 3, Section 2.2 of your Study Text

45. **B** GDP is the value of all goods and service produced in an economy

See Chapter 1, Section 1.9.1 of your Study Text

46. **C** Individual fund management tends to be more expensive as it offers a tailor-made approach

See Chapter 1, Section 3.8 of your Study Text

47. **C** £325,000 is described as the nil rate band (also known as the exempt band). An estate in excess of this level will attract inheritance tax at a rate of 40% on the portion above £325,000

See Chapter 8, Section 3.1 of your Study Text

48. **B** A takeover is a situation where one company acquires another company

See Chapter 2, Section 3.5 of your Study Text

49. **A** FSMA 2000 s118 contains the legislation regarding market abuse

See Chapter 7, Section 4.3 of your Study Text

50. **A** An appropriate definition of insider trading

See Chapter 7, Section 4.1 of your Study Text

Practice Examination 5

50 Questions in 1 Hour

1. Which of the following is a type of order in SETS?

   A   Fill or eliminate

   B   Kill or eliminate

   Ⓒ   At best

   D   Bid

2. Which of the following trading systems do FTSE 100 stocks trade on?

   Ⓐ   SETS

   B   IOB

   C   SETSqx

   D   NASDAQ

3. An investor bought £4,000 nominal value 5% Treasury stock for £3,900. Ignoring tax, how much would he get as his next semi-annual interest payment?

   A   £66.76

   Ⓑ   £100.00

   C   £200.00

   D   £300.00

4. Which of the following is the advantage of the Central Counterparty Service (CCS)?

   A   It allows real-time trading

   B   It allows trading in virt-x to take place

   Ⓒ   It allows trading to be anonymous

   D   It allows for quicker settlement

5. What percentage of those voting must vote in favour for a special resolution to be passed?

   A   50%

   B   55%

   Ⓒ   75%

   D   80%

6. ✗ **Which of the following best describes a form of tax-efficient saving for a higher rate taxpayer?**

   (A) Contributions to a whole-of-life policy

   B Contributions to a stakeholder pension plan

   C Contributions to an investment trust

   D Contributions to a unit trust

7. ✓ **A contract that gives the buyer the obligation to pay for the underlying equity on a specified future date is known as**

   A A call

   B A put

   (C) A future

   D A swap

8. ✓ **Which of the following is true of the way that UK interest rates are set?**

   A Interest rates are set by the Monetary Policy Committee, in line with the European Central Bank's interest rate policy

   (B) Interest rates are set by the Monetary Policy Committee after considering inflation targets set by the Government

   C Interest rates are set by the Government

   D Interest rates are set by the Debt Management Office

9. ✓ **Which of the following is a feature of the ordinary share?**

   A They provide lower risk

   (B) They carry voting rights

   C They pay a predetermined interest rate

   D They are repaid at a future date

10. ✓ **Who is responsible for the safekeeping of assets in an OEIC?**

   (A) Depository

   B Authorised Corporate Director

   C Trustee

   D Manager

11. ✓ **A contract that gives the holder the right to sell an underlying equity is known as**

   A A call

   (B) A put

   C A future

   D A forward

12. On which of the following markets are transactions described as 'spot'?

   A Equity

   B Gilts

   C Foreign exchange

   D Derivatives

13. Which of the following is not an attribute of ordinary shares in a company?

   A The right to vote at company meetings

   B The right to receive a dividend

   C The right of first refusal when new shares are issued

   D The right to receive an equal claim on liquidation of a company, once all other claimants have been paid

14. Breaches of the Data Protection Act 1998 are punishable by

   A Six months' imprisonment and a £5,000 fine

   B Seven years' imprisonment and an unlimited fine

   C Unlimited fines

   D A maximum fine of £100,000 plus costs

15. Which of the following types of behaviour is not included under the market abuse regime?

   A Dealing based on unavailable information

   B Conduct likely to create a misleading impression in the market

   C Behaviour likely to distort the market

   D Abusing the right to transfer data to a country outside the EEA

16. Which of the following is the minimum quote size for a market maker?

   A Large market size

   B Normal market size

   C Smallest market size

   D Average market size

17. According to the DMO classification, Treasury 8% 2015 is

   A A medium

   B A long

   C A short

   D A terminal

18. With whom would it normally be possible to deal in unit trust units?

(A) Trustee

B Custodian

C Intermediary

D Directly with another investor

19. All of the following are examples of tradeable fixed income securities, except

A Yankee bonds

B Gilts

C Convertible bonds

(D) Premium bonds

20. The term 'pre-emptive rights' describes

A Offering shares to new shareholders prior to their general market release

(B) Offering existing shareholders the right to buy new shares before others

C Offering directors of the company shares at a price below that charged to the general public

D Offering shares to only those who have held shares since the initial launch by the company

21. A bond is issued in a country other than that of the issuer is known as a

A Domestic bond

B Strippable bond

(C) Eurobond

D Government bond

22. The CPI is used to measure

(A) Changes in interest rates

B Changes in prices

C Value of sterling

D Standard variable rate on mortgages

23. For an investor under 50 years old, what is the maximum amount that can be invested in a cash ISA in the fiscal year 2010/11?

A £1,800

B £3,600

(C) £5,100

D £7,200

24. ✓ **Which of the following instruments are generally considered to be derivatives?**

    A   Futures and forex

    Ⓑ   Futures and options

    C   Options and forex

    D   Options and convertibles

25. ˣ **Which of the following describes one of the statutory objectives of the FSA?**

    A   Reduce intervention in UK financial markets

    B̲   Reduce the scope for financial crime

    C   Increase understanding of financial regulations

    Ⓓ   Ensure a standard level of protection for all types of investor

26. ₓ **Which of the following bodies is responsible for the listing of equities in the UK?**

    A   Department for Business, Innovation and Skills

    B   Office of Fair Trading

    Ⓒ   London Stock Exchange

    D̲   Financial Services Authority

27. ✓ **Which two of the following are markets on the London Stock Exchange?**

    I   Primary

    II   Secondary

    III   Derivatives

    IV   Commodity

    A   I and IV

    B   II and III

    Ⓒ   I and II

    D   II and IV

28. ✓ **Which of the following best describes the three stages of money laundering?**

    A   Initiation, withdrawal, termination

    B   Integration, investment, withdrawal

    Ⓒ   Placement, layering, integration

    D   Initiation, layering, integration

29. ✓ **Which one of the following statements regarding cash investments is false?**

    Ⓐ   Child trust funds allow a maximum of £15,000 to be invested over a five-year period

    B   Interest paid by banks and building societies generally has tax deducted at source

    C   Cash investments are low risk investments

    D   The maximum that can be subscribed to an ISA is £10,200 in the 2010/11 tax year

30. As a borrower, which of the following rates provides the most useful information?

    A   The quoted rate
    B   The negotiated rate
    C   The AER
    D   The ADR

31. The stage of money laundering that describes the process where the original source of funds is disguised is called

    A   Layering
    B   Integration
    C   Termination
    D   Placement

32. In 2000, the Euronext market was formed from which of the following markets?

    A   Amsterdam, Brussels and Milan
    B   Amsterdam, Brussels and Paris
    C   Brussels, Paris and Frankfurt
    D   Amsterdam, Brussels and Frankfurt

33. In which of the following circumstances is a certificated security deemed to be delivered?

    A   By book entry transfer
    B   The certificate and a signed transfer form are sent to the buyer
    C   The signed stock transfer form is sent to the buyer
    D   By confirming the details of the holding with the register

34. Which of the following is exempt from CGT on its disposal?

    A   Antiques
    B   Cars
    C   Stamp collection
    D   Second home

35. An investment trust has the purpose of

    A   Investing in all type of financial assets
    B   Providing a growing capital sum
    C   Providing a growing level of income
    D   Investing in the shares of other companies

36. Shares in investment trusts are purchased by an investor in a similar way to the purchase of

    A   OEICs

    (B) Equities

    C   Unit trusts

    D   Commodities

37. How many shares make up the Xetra Dax Index?

    (A) 30

    B   33

    C   100

    D   250

38. Which of the following types of mortgage would probably be most suitable for a homeowner expecting general interest rates to fall in the future?

    (A) ISA mortgages

    B   Unit-linked mortgages

    C   Endowment mortgage

    D   Variable rate repayment mortgage

39. Calculate the flat yield on the following bond: Treasury 6% 2011, when it is trading at £120.

    (A) 5.0%

    B   6.0%

    C   5.5%

    D   6.5%

40. Where are the rules governing a company's relationship with the outside world found?

    A   Director's Model Code

    B   Articles of Association

    C   Listing Rules

    (D) Memorandum of Association

41. Which of the following is not a characteristic of Treasury bills?

    A   Issued by DMO

    (B) Pay interest referenced to LIBOR notes

    C   Normal maturity is 91 days

    D   Sold in minimum denominations of £25,000

42. ✗ **In excess of which amount will gains attract capital gains tax in the fiscal year 2010/2011?**

   A   £2,440

   Ⓑ   £6,475

   C   £10,200

   D   £10,100

43. ✓ **Which of the following products would be most suitable for an investor wishing to insure against the risk of death during a specific period?**

   A   Whole of life policy

   B   Unit linked policy

   Ⓒ   Term policy

   D   ISA linked policy

44. ✓ **An investor originally sells a long gilt future and three weeks later buys back the same contract. He is said to have**

   A   Gone long

   B   Exercised his option

   Ⓒ   Closed out his position

   D   Engaged in a swap transaction

45. ✓ **If you want to see capital growth in your investment, which one of the following would you most likely buy?**

   Ⓐ   Equities

   B   Gilts

   C   Warrants

   D   Options

46. ✗ **Which of the following bodies is responsible for enforcing anti-money laundering legislation within the authorised community?**

   A   FSA

   Ⓑ   FSCS

   C   SOCA

   D   HM Treasury

47. ✗ **An investor buys a gilt for £96.78 and holds it until maturity when it redeems at £100. How much will the investor pay in capital gains tax?**

   A   Nothing

   B   £3.22

   Ⓒ   18% of £3.22 (the capital gain)

   D   It depends on the investor's marginal tax rate

48. ✕ **The period which runs from the 6 April in one year to the 5 April in the next is known as the**

    Ⓐ Financial year

    B Fiscal year

    C Accounting year

    D None of the above

49. ✓ **Who would report a suspicious transaction to the Serious Organised Crime Agency?**

    A The employee directly

    Ⓑ The MLRO of the firm

    C The firm's executive committee

    D The JMSLG after consulting with the firm's compliance department

50. ✕ **Which one of the following statements is true?**

    Ⓐ The personal allowance for income tax for the fiscal year 2010/11 is £10,100

    B The rate of VAT on newspapers is 5%

    C The personal allowance of £6,475 cannot be carried forward to another tax year

    D Stamp duty payable by the seller of shares is 0.5% rounded up to the nearest £5

Answers

1.   **C**   The other order types are limit, execute and eliminate, fill or kill, market

   See Chapter 2, Section 7.3 of your Study Text

2.   **A**   FTSE 100 stocks trade on SETS

   See Chapter 2, Section 7.1 of your Study Text

3.   **B**   The semi-annual payment is

   Nominal value × 5% × ½

   = £4,000 × 5% × ½

   = £100

   See Chapter 2, Section 10.2.4 of your Study Text

4.   **C**   This is the best available answer. The CCS allows novation to occur, thus trades are anonymous on SETS. Settlement is likely to be more efficient but not necessarily quicker

   See Chapter 2, Section 7.2 of your Study Text

5.   **C**   75% of those voting must vote in favour

   See Chapter 2, Section 1.3 of your Study Text

6.   **B**   Tax relief is offered on contributions to pension plans at the taxpayer's marginal rate of tax

   See Chapter 4, Section 3.7 of your Study Text

7.   **C**   Futures create obligations on both the part of the buyer and seller

   See Chapter 3, Section 2.1 of your Study Text

8.   **B**   Interest rates are set independently by the MPC after considering the inflation target

   See Chapter 1, Section 2.2 of your Study Text

9.   **B**   Ordinary shares carry voting rights, unlike preference shares, which will typically only carry votes if the preference dividend has been in arrears five years or more

   See Chapter 2, Section 1.5 of your Study Text

10.   **A**   A depository performs the same function of safekeeping in an OEIC as the trustees of a unit trust. The Authorised Corporate Director is the manager of an OEIC

   See Chapter 5, Section 3.2 of your Study Text

11.   **B**   The right to sell an underlying equity is known as a put option

   See Chapter 3, Section 3.1 of your Study Text

12.   **C**   Transactions on the foreign exchange market for immediate trades at the current price are called 'spot' transactions

   See Chapter 1, Section 7.2 of your Study Text

13. **B** There is no automatic right to receive a dividend. The approach is rather that all ordinary shareholders will participate equally if a dividend is declared

See Chapter 2, Section 2.1.2 of your Study Text

14. **C** This would be a Crown Court sanction. The maximum fine in a Magistrates' Court would be £5,000

See Chapter 7, Section 5 of your Study Text

15. **D** Transferring data outside the EEA, unless that country has adequate protection of rights of data subjects, is a breach of data protection law (Data Protection Act 1998) and does not fall within the market abuse regime

See Chapter 7, Sections 4.3 and 5 of your Study Text

16. **B** Normal Market Size is the minimum size that a market maker must quote to, although they may quote higher

See Chapter 2, Section 2.8.1 of your Study Text

17. **C** A gilt with less than seven years' run is called a short, according to the DMO classifications

See Chapter 2, Section 10.4 of your Study Text

18. **C** You could place an order through an intermediary (IFS or tied agent) and they, in turn, would deal with the fund manager

See Chapter 5, Section 2.5 of your Study Text

19. **D** Premium Bonds are offered by National Savings & Investments and are not tradeable. All the other instruments may be kept until maturity or sold on into the market

See Chapter 2, Section 11 of your Study Text

20. **B** It is the right of existing shareholders to be offered the rights shares issued by the company, prior to others

See Chapter 2, Section 2.1.5 of your Study Text

21. **C** Eurobonds are normally issued in a country other than that of the issuer. The currency of issue does not link to the country it is issued in

See Chapter 2, Section 11.1 of your Study Text

22. **B** The Consumer Price Index measures the increase in prices of a fixed basket of goods and, therefore, inflation

See Chapter 1, Section 1.8.1 of your Study Text

23. **C** The maximum that can be invested in a cash ISA is £5,100 for 2010/11. There are no longer different limits according to age

See Chapter 3, Section 3.3 of your Study Text

24. **B** Futures and options derive their value from an underlying asset and refer to a deferred delivery at a future date. Forex is a phrase used to describe foreign exchange and covers both spot or immediate transactions and forwards, which are similar in nature to futures

See Chapter 3, Section 1 of your Study Text

25. **B**   Reduction of financial crime is one of the four statutory objectives of FSMA 2000

     See Chapter 7, Section 2.2 of your Study Text

26. **D**   The UK Listing Authority (UKLA) is responsible as the Competent Authority, and this is part of the FSA

     See Chapter 2, Section 4 of your Study Text

27. **C**   The primary and secondary markets are aspects of the London Stock Exchange

     See Chapter 1, Sections 4.2 and 4.3 of your Study Text

28. **C**   Placement, layering and integration is the best answer

     See Chapter 7, Section 3.2 of your Study Text

29. **A**   The maximum that could be invested in a CTF is £1,200 pa for 18 years

     See Chapter 6, Section 2 of your Study Text

30. **C**   The AER or Annual Equivalent Rate takes into account any charges the borrower is likely to pay and, thus, represents a more complete picture of how much the loan really costs

     See Chapter 4, Section 5 of your Study Text

31. **A**   Layering describes the process whereby money is moved around the financial system to try to hide its origin. Placement is when the money is first put in and Integration is when the money, now seemingly legitimate, is taken out

     See Chapter 7, Section 3.2 of your Study Text

32. **B**   The Euronext market was formed from the exchanges of Amsterdam, Paris and Brussels. The Lisbon exchange is now also part of Euronext

     See Chapter 1, Section 6.2 of your Study Text

33. **B**   Delivery occurs when the old share certificate and signed stock transfer form are completed by the seller

     See Chapter 2, Sections 2.3 and 9.6 of your Study Text

34. **B**   Cars (considered to be wasting assets) and the main home are exempt from CGT

     See Chapter 8, Section 2.2 of your Study Text

35. **D**   Investment trusts invest in the shares of other companies

     See Chapter 5, Section 4.1 of your Study Text

36. **B**   Shares in investment trusts are purchased in the same way as equities since both are quoted on the LSE

     See Chapter 5, Section 4.2 of your Study Text

37. **A**   The Xetra Dax represents the top 30 German shares

     See Chapter 2, Section 6.2 of your Study Text

38. **D** A mortgage with a variable rate means that the interest varies in line with the general interest rate climate and, thus, would represent a lower interest rate cost when rates fall

   See Chapter 4, Section 6.3 of your Study Text

39. **A** The flat yield id calculated as follows.

   $$\text{Flat yield} = \frac{\text{Gross Coupon}}{\text{Market price}} \times 100$$

   $$= \frac{£6}{£120} \times 100$$

   $$= 5\%$$

   See Chapter 2, Section 11.7 of your Study Text

40. **D** Each company has two constitutional documents. The Memorandum of Association is the external rulebook of the company, governing its relationship with the outside world. The Articles of Association is the internal rulebook governing the relationship between the company and its shareholders

   See Chapter 2, Section 1.2.1 of your Study Text

41. **B** Treasury bills do not pay interest. Instead, they trade at a discount to face value

   See Chapter 2, Section 12.2 of your Study Text

42. **D** The annual CGT exemption which is granted on a 'use it or lose it' basis (£10,200 is the maximum amount that can be invested in an ISA in any one fiscal year)

   See Chapter 8, Section 2.3 of your Study Text

43. **C** Term assurance covers against the risk of death occurring during a specified term only, whereas whole-of-life policies pay out on death, whenever that happens

   See Chapter 4, Section 7 of your Study Text

44. **C** Taking the equal but opposite position from the original position is called 'closing out' and effectively extinguishes the obligation to make delivery of the asset at the agreed price and date

   See Chapter 3, Section 2.2 of your Study Text

45. **A** Equities or shares offer the investor both potential income from dividends and capital growth over time. These are seen as investments for long-term growth

   See Chapter 2, Section 2.1.3 of your Study Text

46. **A** All FSA-authorised firms must follow the anti-money laundering legislation as set out and it is the FSA that will primarily investigate any breaches

   See Chapter 7, Section 3 of your Study Text

47. **A** Remember that gilts are exempt from capital gains tax. However, the coupon is subject to income tax at the investor's marginal tax rate

   See Chapter 8, Section 2.2 of your Study Text

48. **B** The financial year runs from 1 April to 31 March the following year

    See Chapter 8, Section 1.2 of your Study Text

49. **B** The MLRO of the firm

    See Chapter 7, Section 3.3 of your Study Text

50. **C** The personal allowance is granted on a use-it-or-lose-it basis. Newspapers are zero-rated for VAT. Only buyers pay stamp duty on share transactions

    See Chapter 8. Sections 1.3 of your Study Text